Praise for *The CoParenting Toolkit*

Dr. Ricci has done it again! *The CoParenting Toolkit* **will likely become the resource manual for co-parents, their attorneys, and mediators** trying to navigate the complexities of coparenting in today's world. The practical recommendations and hints for success are worth the price of the book. The vignettes help parents know there are others who have similar, yet solvable problems. Kids' Turn is pleased to recommend this to families enrolled in our services.

—Claire N. Barnes, MA
Executive Director, Kids' Turn

Best I have seen in this kind of book! Isolina Ricci has managed to get more useful and practical information in fewer pages than any other author on this topic. It's actually *fun* **to read.** *The CoParenting Toolkit* is easy on the eye, and the layout allows readers to digest material rapidly. This book is a fit for a high school level reader or a professor in psychology—and that is hard to accomplish. I am looking forward to distributing this book to my colleagues in the family court and parent education.

—Phillip Reedy, MA
Family Court Mediator, former Education
Coordinator, California Statewide Office of
Family Court Services

In this new book, **Isolina Ricci provides a rich, concise, and highly readable manual for parents** coping with the difficult process of coparenting after divorce. She expands upon ideas presented in her classic book, *Mom's House, Dad's House*, by giving parents specific guidelines to help them navigate the confusing process of learning how to negotiate parenting together after divorce. In a reader-friendly format, Dr. Ricci helps parents define their goals and provides them with tools that will make coparenting work for them. **This is an excellent resource that belongs on the shelves of all professionals who work with divorced parents.**

—Constance Ahrons, Ph.D.
Author of *The Good Divorce* and *We're Still Family*

The CoParenting Toolkit **is one of those books you hope every single parent and coparent will read and use. It's practical, inspiring, and easy-to-use.** The Quizzes and Guidelines were my favorites.

—Linda Delbar, BSN, School Nurse (retired)

Divorce is a maelstrom with potentially devastating consequences for both parents and children. Isolina Ricci's *CoParenting Toolkit* provides an eminently do-able set of steps to help calm the storm and create a constructive parenting plan for the whole family's benefit. **This is an enormous contribution to the cause of effective parenting and the well-being of the children of divorce.**

—Jeff Gillenkirk, author of *Home, Away*

The CoParenting Toolkit **is a very helpful book. Parents will appreciate Dr. Ricci's kindly encouragement, practical tips, and wise advice.** After reading this book parents will understand the meaning of coparenting and be better prepared to decide whether or how it might work for them and their children.

—Professor Nancy Ver Steegh,
William Mitchell College of Law

Dr. Ricci continues to offer practical, positive structures for parents. **Toolkit is also a map to new parenting destinations** and can be kept close-at-hand while the new routes are learned.

—Hon. Susan Snow, (Ret), Family Law Judge,
Past-President of Association of Family and
Conciliation Courts

The classic guide people return to again and again

Often called "the bible", this is the comprehensive guide for separated, divorced, and remarried parents. The latest edition has 5 more chapters and 100 additional pages on custody, schedules, dealing with the other parent, mediation, Parenting Plans, meeting children's needs, building your family, long-distance parenting, making tough times work for you, and much more. This book is your friend.

20 Chapters, 8 Appendices, 381 pages.

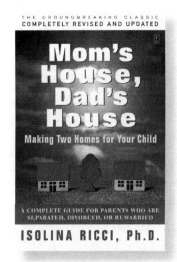

This book should be a required textbook for every divorcing parent.
—Michael J. Ostrow, Past President, American Academy of Matrimonial Lawyers

For kids and their parents
on separation, divorce, stepfamilies and staying strong.

This wonderful book is a quick but important read for parents, a lifesaving handbook for kids. Get an inside look at what kids really want, need, do, and say, about separation, stepfamilies, and how to believe in themselves. Alive with examples, stories, tips, maps. Designed to reduce anxiety, encourage self-esteem, resiliency, and family teamwork.

12 Chapters plus worksheets. 271 pages.

The HOW-TO BOOK OF THE WEEK,
—Newsday, May 22, 2006

Read reviews at www.momshousedadshouse.com
Available at all local and online bookstores

The CoParenting TOOLKIT

The CoParenting TOOLKIT

The Essential Supplement for *Mom's House, Dad's House*

Isolina Ricci, Ph.D.

author of
Mom's House, Dad's House
Mom's House, Dad's House for Kids

Custody & CoParenting Solutions
custodyandcoparentingsolutions.com
San Ramon, California

The CoParenting Toolkit:
The Essential Supplement for Mom's House, Dad's House
Copyright © 2012 by Isolina Ricci
Published by Custody and CoParenting Solutions
San Ramon, California

ISBN-13: 978-0-9827295-0-2 (B&W Edition)

Book Design: DesignForBooks.com
Editorial & Publishing: EricksonEditorial.net

WEBSITES
thecoparentingtoolkit.com
custodyandcoparentingsolutions.com

FOR PROFESSIONALS
Trainings and Workshops
Toolkit Guide

SCHOOLS
Lesson Plans
Author Visits

PARENT EDUCATION
Study Guides
Teaching Manuals

A Publication of
Custody & CoParenting Solutions

Contents

● ● ● ● ● ● ● ● ● ● ● ● ●

Before You Begin   ix

Introduction   1

What's Best for Children?   1

Tools for Your Success   2

Quiz: What Do You Have to Work with Today?   3

The Heart of CoParenting Is Commitment   4

How to Use This Toolkit   6

Use the CoParenting Highway's Basic Guidelines   9

From Live-Together Parenting to Mom's House, Dad's House   9

The CoParenting Highway   10

Basic Guidelines for CoParenting   11

Tips for Using the Basic CoParenting Guidelines   13

How CoParenting Guidelines Can Help Avoid Hassles   16

Switch Lanes for More Flexible or More Limited CoParenting   19

Flexible CoParenting—The Left Lane   19

Flexible Guidelines for CoParenting   20

Tips for Flexible CoParenting   21

Limited CoParenting—The Right Lane   23

Limited CoParenting Guidelines   24

Tips For Limited CoParenting   27

Dangers of Long-Term Limited CoParenting   31

Your Own Combination of CoParenting Guidelines   32

Use Your Strengths and Set Your Course   35

Use Your Strengths   35

Quiz: What Are Your Strengths?   36

What Do You Want for Your Child?   38

Quiz: What Worries You?   40

Wakeup Calls   41

Speed Healing by Managing Hurt and Hard Feelings   45

When Hard Feelings Spill Over into CoParenting   46

How to Start Building (and Stop Bleeding)   46

Negative Intimacy—The Dark Side   48

Quiz: Your Negative Intimacy Inventory   51

How to Manage Negative Intimacy and Get Back in Control   52

Use Special Business Guidelines for Relating to the Other Parent   57

How to Be "Business-Like"   57

Parent-Business Guidelines   58

Tips for Following the Guidelines   59

Tips on How to Get Along with the Other Parent   61

What Are Your Personal Boundaries?   62

Grief and Grieving—It's Not Easy but Necessary   64

Getting to a Relaxed Business Relationship   65

Try These Tools to Side-Step Communication Potholes   69

Keep Each Other Up to Date   69

Guidelines for Effective CoParent Communication   70

Prepare for Meetings and Emails   72

Manage Your Stress   73

Guidelines for Limited CoParenting Communication   74

Acknowledge the Other Parent's Strengths   76

Guidelines for E-Etiquette 78

Avoid the Miserable Middle for You and the Kids 81

The Miserable Middle—No Way Out 81

Eavesdropping, Telling Tales, Lying, Refereeing 82

Quiz: Are Children in the Middle? 84

When Kids Say Things That Raise a Red Flag 85

Handling the Red Flags with Your Child 86

Avoiding Negative Intimacy Traps 87

Trouble or Teamwork 89

Boost Your Skills for Solving Problems 91

Steps to Reaching Agreements 92

Example: The Yearly Time-Share Schedule 95

Example: Choosing a High School 98

Your Problem-Solving Style 101

Find Ways to Help Your Child 105

Things Kids Want Parents to Know 106

What Parents Can Do to Help Their Child 107

Going Back and Forth Between Homes 108

House and Safety Rules 110

What Do You Want for Your Child? 113

Fine Tune Your Parenting Style 117

Consider Your Parenting Style 117

Guidelines for the "Developmental" Parenting Style 121

Your Child's Temperament and Moving 124

Parenting Checklist 125

Put Together a First-Rate Parenting Plan 127

A Useful and Solid Legal Plan 127

What Do You Have Now? 128

What Can Go into Parenting Plans   129

Other Things to Consider   130

Optional Private Agreements   132

The "Who Does What" List   134

What Would You Do?   135

Design a Winning and Workable Family Schedule   139

A Winning and Workable Parenting Schedule   139

Your Child's Temperament   140

Sharing Time with Your Child   141

Designing Your Schedule   142

How Some Parents Share Time   146

When More Overnights Are Not the Answer   147

More Secrets to Successful Scheduling   151

Epilogue   155

Appendices

Appendix   1   *Never-Married CoParents   159*

Appendix   2   *Parenting Plans, Online Resources, and Referrals   160*

Appendix   3   *Safety Rules   163*

Appendix   4   *House Rules   165*

Appendix   5   *Example List of Family Values   169*

Appendix   6   *Holiday Tips for Separated or Divorced Parents and Blended Families   170*

Appendix   7   *When and When Not to Use the "I" Message   172*

Appendix   8   *Important Phone Numbers, Safety and Emergency Hotlines   174*

Appendix   9   *When You Have Done All You Can Do   175*

Appendix   10   *The Bookshelf   177*

Thank You   179

About the Author   180

AUTHOR'S NOTE: The new and expanded tools and guidelines in this book are taken from the author's workshops for professionals and her work with families since the publication of the second edition of **Mom's House, Dad's House** in 1997. For a history of the **Mom's House, Dad's House** concepts beginning in 1974, see the *Chapter Notes* and *References* in the first and second editions.

Before You Begin

• • • • • • • • • • • • • • • • • • •

Welcome to *The CoParenting Toolkit*, an easy-to-use guide designed for today's busy parent. It's the essential add-on for the comprehensive classic, *Mom's House, Dad's House* and its partner for parents and children, *Mom's House, Dad's House for KIDS*.

These first books embrace those universal heartbreaks, betrayals, conflicts, and dilemmas that invariably touch relationships and families in each generation. They offer time-tested and commonsense strategies and solutions that parents and their children use successfully to this day. Now, there is even more research and experience to fold in. That's why *The CoParenting Toolkit* was written. It adds to these first books, but it doesn't replace them.

This toolkit expands and deepens some of the time-tested solutions from the first books and then adds a series of fresh new strategies for today. It's packed with step-by-step explanations, realistic examples, Guidelines, useful checklists, Quizzes, worksheets, and quotes from parents sharing their wisdom. Its mission is the same as the *Mom's House, Dad's House* books before it—to support you and your children before, during, and after you separate.

Before you begin reading this book, read the section below, "Is CoParenting Right for You Now?" Coparenting can be the best option for many families but for those who struggle with serious problems or allegations, coparenting may not be healthy or realistic right now. This section can help you decide.

Coparenting is a respectful partnership between parents living apart who work together to love, protect, and raise their child.

IS COPARENTING RIGHT FOR YOU NOW?

Take a look at the questions on the following page. If they don't apply to you, just skip these pages and go to the Introduction. Sorry to say, the list of questions is not a happy one, but some parents do have to deal with these situations. It's best to think about these issues right up front in order to decide if traditional coparenting is right for you *at this time*.

If the situations below don't apply to you, skip this page and go to the Introduction.

✓ Difficult Situations for You or the Other Parent

	NO	SOME	YES
1. Do you feel that your child is not safe left alone with the other parent or with others who either live with or hang around the other parent?	○	○	○
2. Are there problems with drugs, marijuana, or alcohol abuse?	○	○	○
3. Do you have serious concerns about the other parent's ability to care for a child because of serious physical or mental health issues such as suicide attempts, severe depression, or debilitating disease?	○	○	○
4. Are you worried about the other parent's harassment, need for revenge, or stalking?	○	○	○

What about These Dangerous Situations?

	NO	SOME	YES
5. Have there been verbal or physical abuse or threats?	○	○	○
6. Have there been arrests, incarcerations, or criminal litigation?	○	○	○
7. Has there been a child protective services investigation for alleged neglect, or physical or sexual abuse?	○	○	○
8. Has there been a situation where there were weapons, injury, or where the police were called?	○	○	○
9. Is there now or has there been over the past five years, a restraining order because of domestic violence, harassment, stalking, abuse, or threats?	○	○	○
10. Do you think the other parent would say he or she has any of the above concerns about you?	○	○	○

How to Use Your Answers

"No" answers are good signs. Nothing can guarantee that a coparenting relationship today will be healthy for your child, but you don't believe you have these serious difficulties and roadblocks.

"Yes" or "Some" answers to any of these questions suggest that you or the other parent have legal and safety issues around custody that say coparenting is not a good idea for now. Things aren't always as they seem and sometimes a parent is falsely accused or detained. Still, these answers may mean that trying to coparent in the traditional way may not be right for your child. In some states, there are laws that prohibit custody or unsupervised visitation in certain circumstances, so don't count on this book for answers to your own legal situation.

Get some expert advice where you live. You may be able to work with an attorney or another legal professional to find safe ways for both parents to be involved in parenting, even if it is restricted in some ways and one parent or a guardian has full custody.

> **Question:** What if I answered "no" to all the questions, but the other parent isn't interested or has basically dropped out of the children's lives?
>
> **Answer:** While there are many good tools in this book, none of them can guarantee that the other parent will become an active and positive parent if you are the only one using these tools. We can't change other people. They have to change on their own. Instead, concentrate on what can make things better for you and your children. If in the future, the other parent does show interest in coparenting, then you could be be better prepared to help shape a good relationship with him or her. In the next chapter, check out the section "How to Use This Toolkit."

 IMPORTANT

If you do have any of these difficulties *don't count on books, the Internet, or TV experts for the final word on your situation. Talk face-to-face with a licensed counselor, an attorney, or both. Pick someone who knows your local court and state laws.*

Introduction

. . . .

What's Best for Children?
Tools for Your Success
Quiz: What Do You Have to Work with Today?
The Heart of CoParenting Is Commitment
How to Use This Toolkit

Dear Parent,

Chances are that you have picked up this book because you and your children's other parent are not living together. You deeply love your child and you probably share the same hope, along with millions of other loving parents who live apart, that you can still give your children what they need to grow up strong, healthy, and happy. Maybe you are just starting your coparenting journey and are looking for guidelines and ideas on how it can work. Perhaps you already have a coparenting relationship and are wondering if there are more ways to either improve it or protect what you have now. Or you are familiar with the *Mom's House, Dad's House* books and want to know about the latest developments. Well, you've all come to the right place. This *Toolkit* can help.

WHAT'S BEST FOR CHILDREN?

You probably have already heard that after separation, children can do well if they have both parents in their lives. Often, this is taken to mean that each parent has a substantial amount of parenting time and that they share decision making. But while these are important, these alone won't help children thrive. How well children manage can depend more on other things parents do or don't do. For example, hard feelings between parents, especially when children observe or hear them, are very toxic for children (not to mention for the parents). This is true whether or not parents share parenting time and decisions. There are other influences of course, like personalities, finances, neighborhoods, living conditions, just to mention a few, but in my experience it is how well you parent and how well you coparent that are at the top of the list. Luckily, these are all things we can do, build up, repair, or learn!

Lovers may come and go, but your relationship with your child is for life.

The Goal of Healthy CoParenting Is for You and Your Child to Thrive

Healthy coparenting should give you and your child the chance to thrive, not just cope. It is more than setting up two homes and a schedule. It is also about how you build a life for yourself and your child, your relationship with the other parent, and your individual relationships with your children. As coparents, you'll be solving problems, communicating, networking, making decisions, settling disagreements, and hopefully building a strong coparent team. This *Toolkit* and the *Mom's House, Dad's House* books were written exactly for these situations.

TOOLS FOR YOUR SUCCESS

What Are These Tools?

In this book, "tools" are a selection of tips, strategies, ideas, quizzes, lists, guidelines, and checklists that have helped many people with different situations over more than 30 years. Each chapter will have one or more things for you to try. Some tools amplify those in *Mom's House, Dad's House* while many others are relatively new. You can count on at least some of the tools in this *Toolkit* to give you some ideas and options.

You Already Know a Lot

You probably use your own version of some tools in this book for your everyday life already. But coparenting often means "re-tooling" or retrofitting ways we act. For example, you know that you have to communicate with the other parent, but with coparenting you'll learn there are certain words you can choose to get your point across instead of other words which could shut things down. You'll find specifics about these words in *Chapter 6: Try These Tools to Side-Step Communication Potholes*. Knowing the best words to use is one of the important adjustments for effective coparenting.

Perfect coparenting is not realistic. Instead, set your sights on your "best possible" type of coparenting. Make it good enough so that it helps you and your child thrive, not just survive.

Coparenting often means "re-tooling" or retrofitting ways we act as parents.

This is a very important quiz. Please don't skip this one. Your answers can give you an idea of the foundation for coparenting that you have to work with right now, today. Don't be surprised if you want to change your answers later. Just thinking about things can start a chain reaction of behavior changes.

When you answer these questions, give a separate answer for each child.

✓ What Do You Have to Work with Today?

	YES	NOT SURE	PROBABLY NOT
1. Do you think the other parent loves your child and wants to be an active parent?	✓	○	○
2. Do you think your child is securely bonded or attached to the other parent?	✓	○	○
3. Do you think your child needs or wants the other parent active in his or her life?	✓	○	○
4. Do you think the other parent can put your child's needs first?	○	✓	○
5. Do you trust the other parent to take good care of your child?	✓	○	○
6. Is it important to you that your child has a good relationship with the other parent?	✓	○	○
7. Are you committed to making your best effort to have a healthy coparenting relationship?	✓	○	○
8. Do you think the other parent wants you to have a close relationship with your child?	✓	○	○
9. Do you think the other parent will make his or her best effort to have a healthy coparenting relationship?	○-✓-○		○

How to Use Your Answers

Your "Yes" answers are your most important strengths for coparenting today. These are some of the essentials of commitment. Making coparenting work requires energy and effort, and "Yes" answers are good signs that you can make that commitment. They are all the driving forces that can make coparenting a good experience for you and your child. Give yourself gold stars and protect your strengths.

"Not Sure" answers are your "Slippery Slopes." Pay very close attention to these. If you and the other parent can explore these further and find some solutions, you can eventually make these your strengths, too. If you ignore these, even if you only have one "Not Sure" answer, it may eventually fall into the "Probably Not" category. Read the rest of this book and put some of the tools into action. If your progress is slow, then work with a coparent counselor to untangle what's holding you back.

"Probably Not" answers are your "Red Flags." These are calls to action. If you can still say that you are both committed to making your best effort to have a healthy coparenting relationship, then start working with a coparenting counselor as soon as possible.

THE HEART OF COPARENTING IS COMMITMENT

It can't be said enough. Your most important strengths are your commitment to coparenting and your ability to put your child's needs first. They are the glue that can hold things together when things get shaky. When parents are willing to commit their best efforts to make coparenting succeed, they are well on their way.

Monika and Roberto

Monika, age 28, and Roberto, age 39, lived together for five years and separated three years ago. They have two children, Sam, 8, and Nell, 6. Monika is a former model who is now finishing her degree in education. Roberto is a building contractor who specializes in flipping houses and who coaches Pop Warner football. He has a teenage son from a previous marriage who lives in another state. Roberto reports that he learned his lesson with his first divorce and is doing a better job coparenting this time around. He and Monika answered "Yes" to all the questions with one exception. Roberto said he was "Not Sure" if Monika would give coparenting her best efforts. Up until recently, Roberto would have answered "Yes" to that question, but now Monika is seeing someone seriously, and Roberto has started to feel uneasy. Still, Monika and Roberto do have a strong commitment to their children and to coparenting. These are their biggest strengths for the future.

Commitment and putting your child first is the glue that holds coparenting together.

put kids first
1

Laura and Cody

Laura, age 42, and Cody, age 43, have been living apart for five months. Laura has a lively, forceful personality and runs her own business as a caterer. Cody is a quiet man who works as an engineer with the city. He became involved in an affair two years ago and left Laura to live with his girlfriend, Hanna. Laura filed for divorce last month and they have started working with a mediator to work out their settlement and arrangements for their children: twins Megan and Alicia, 12, and Matt, 4. They want to coparent, but as Cody says, "Every time we try to communicate, it turns into an argument." The good news is that when they took this quiz, they both had all "Yes" answers except for two "Not Sure" answers. Laura wasn't sure that Cody would put the children's needs first before his girlfriend. Cody said he would make his best efforts for a healthy coparenting relationship, but he was not sure Laura would. Despite the affair and their arguments and distrust about the other parent's commitment, these parents still seem to have enough heart and willingness to make coparenting work.

HOW TO USE THIS TOOLKIT

▶ *You don't have to try everything in this Toolkit.* There's enough here to give you plenty of options. If you just choose one idea or action every few weeks, it could help to relieve your stress and guide you toward more success as a coparent.

▶ *Go ahead and skip around from chapter to chapter. But first read about the CoParenting Highway in Chapters 1 and 2.* This can help you focus on what you want from the other chapters.

▶ *Keep this Toolkit as your private copy.* You may want to keep your answers to certain questions confidential. The other parent needs his or her own private copy. Keep this *Toolkit* in a secure place. Your children should not read your answers.

▶ *Share some Worksheets.* You decide which worksheets you fill in by yourself, which you share with the other parent, and which you work on together. You might share some worksheets with your counselor and your attorney since they contain useful information that can help them understand your situation better.

▶ *Dedicate a confidential notebook or journal to your coparenting experience.* You may want to make notes on your feelings or experiences but also your answers to different Quizzes or notes about the various suggested Guidelines.

▶ *If you are parenting alone right now, you may still find some useful tools in this book.* Even though parenting solo is a really tough job, it can also be very rewarding and successful. If you are a solo parent who still has some communications with the other parent and his or her family members, Chapters 4 through 10 may help you set limits, pick tools and strategies for communications, make decisions, and keep strong for yourself and for your children. Ideally, no matter what your circumstances, you have or can build a support group and a sense of community with your friends, church, and extended family.[1] Check out Chapter 11 of this book about Parenting Plans, and certain chapters of *Mom's House, Dad's House*, especially if the absent parent does come back into the picture.[2]

▶ *How to find coparenting counselors, family mediators, and family law attorneys.* In this book, there may be suggestions to talk to

> If you or the other parent can't commit your best efforts today, this doesn't mean that coparenting won't work. It may take longer, or it's not something that can happen right now. Go through this book before you decide.

professionals such as an attorney, a coparent counselor, a family mediator, or others. *Appendix 2: Parenting Plans, Online Resources, and Referrals* has information on how to find referrals in your area. You can also check with the National Counseling Association, American Association of Marriage and Family Therapists, the American Psychological Association, the Family Law Section of the American Bar Association or your State Bar Association, and your state's list of Licensed Clinical Social Workers. You can find referrals for family mediators by asking your counselor or family law attorney for the names of experienced mediators. Often your local Family Service Agency and Legal Aid organizations are able to be of service.

▶ **Do you have any of the Mom's House, Dad's House *books?*** If yes, there are NOTES at the end of each chapter in this *Toolkit* with the exact pages in those books where you can find additional information or the original perspectives.

A final note: To protect the privacy of clients, students, and colleagues who have shared their experiences with me, all names, places, and identifying circumstances of any real people have been changed, and examples are representative composites rather than single cases. Finally, you are the parent and the expert when it comes to your life and your children. This book and the other *Mom's House, Dad's House* books offer options, ideas, and guidelines, but only you can make the decision if these options and suggestions are best for you.

The first chapter starts at a quick pace. It's about the Basic CoParenting Guidelines and the recommended rules of the road for the "CoParenting Highway." Everyone needs to know what to expect from the other parent, and what's expected of them.

It probably took years for you and the other parent to get to where you are now. It will probably take a while to neutralize any hard feelings between you, or at the least to find a detour around them. Try to be patient.

NOTES FOR INTRODUCTION

1. *Chapter 17*, "Your Family Network," in *Mom's House, Dad's House: Making Two Homes for Your Child* can be helpful.

2. In *Mom's House, Dad's House*, there is an entire chapter called "When an Absent Parent Returns: Things to Consider" (pp. 298–306). Also see the five chapters in Part III on the Legal Business in *Mom's House, Dad's House*.

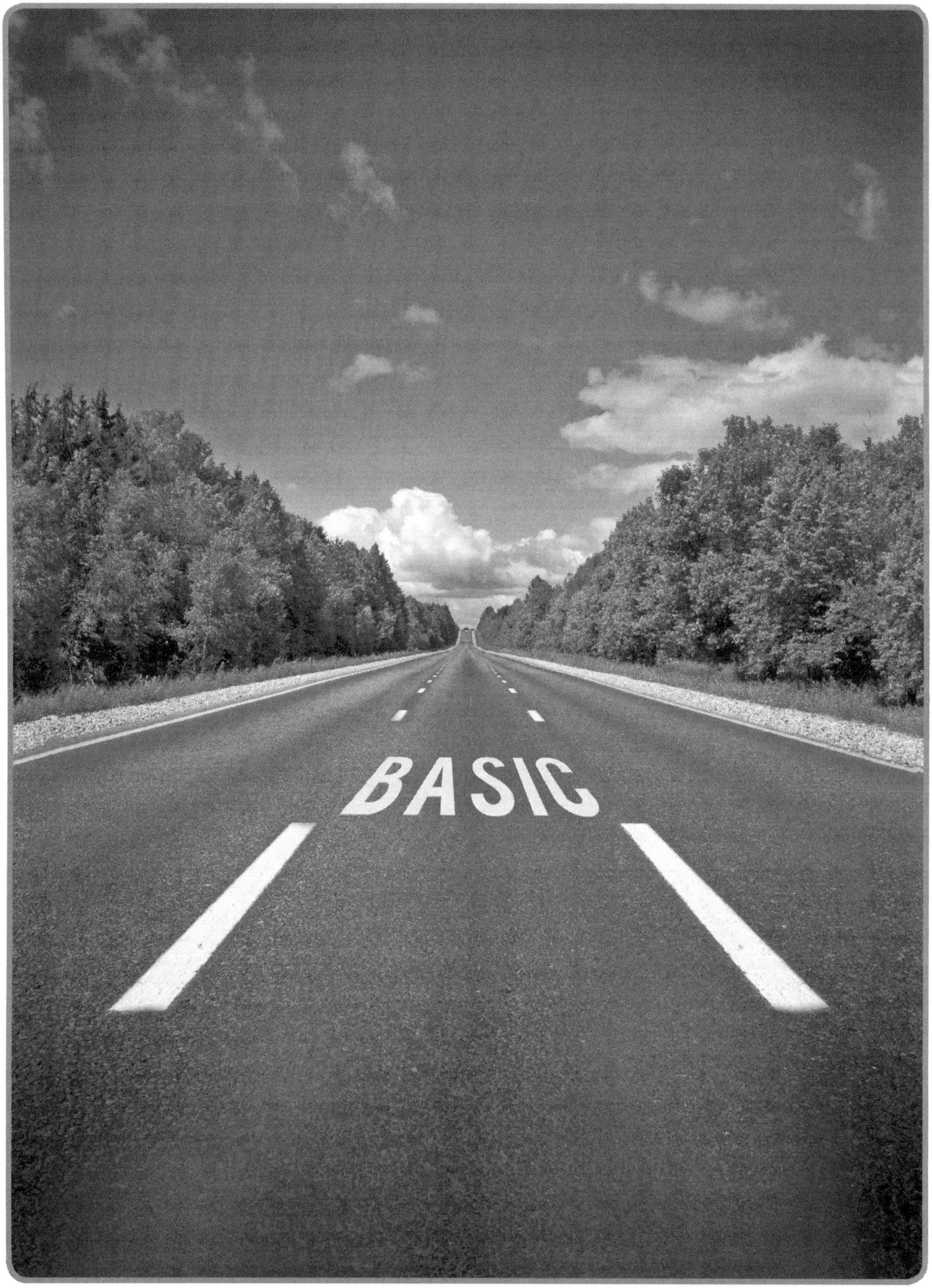
BASIC

1

Use the CoParenting Highway's Basic Guidelines

From Live-Together Parenting to Mom's House, Dad's House
The CoParenting Highway
Basic Guidelines for CoParenting
Tips for Using the CoParenting Guidelines
How CoParenting Guidelines Can Help Avoid Hassles

FROM LIVE-TOGETHER PARENTING TO MOM'S HOUSE, DAD'S HOUSE

Coparenting after separation is more complicated than live-together parenting! It is a *major* lifestyle change. Even though many things about daily life with your kids will seem the same as before, many others are not. When there is just one parent taking on all the responsibility on a given day, there's a lot more to do, even if you are coparenting. On top of all this, you also have to follow the court order, the Parenting Plan (see Chapter 11), try to get along with the other parent, and help your child through this major transition. Whew! It's a lot.

Guidelines to the rescue! This chapter is all about using Basic CoParenting Guidelines to help you on your journey. It's only fair that both of you play by the same rules and that each of you know what to expect. Besides, these Guidelines might also help you avoid some expensive and painful detours while you shape your best possible arrangement for your child. If you are having trouble meeting these Guidelines, check out the next chapter for extra help. If things are going smoothly, the next chapter also has Guidelines with more flexibility. No matter what your situation, the Basic CoParenting Guidelines describe what good-enough, healthy coparenting can look like.

THE COPARENTING HIGHWAY

The Big Center Lane

It can help to picture coparenting as a major highway with three lanes. In this chapter we start with the big center lane—the Basic CoParenting Guidelines. These are the recommended rules of the road for all coparents.

The Basic Guidelines = Common Sense + CoParenting Add-Ons

As you look over the Basic CoParenting Guidelines, you'll see that you already know most of these things anyway because they are common sense and good parenting. The difference is that you now have to adapt them for successful coparenting. One Dad laughed and said, "These are the CoParenting Apps."

Some of these guidelines are not always easy to put into practice, especially at first. No one does them all perfectly. Still, they are all important to try and follow. Just like learning to drive a new car on unfamiliar, unmarked roads, some things can be frustrating at first, but when you stay with it, over time it starts to come together. And just like driving, we don't always drive the way we should even though we know it's safer for everyone. The Guidelines are reminders and aids to improving our habits.

BASIC GUIDELINES

FOR COPARENTING

You as a Parent

- **Put your child first. Love your child more than you dislike or distrust the other parent.**
- **Be sure your child sees and hears you and others being respectful and courteous** with the other parent and the other parent's partner.
- **Make it easy for your child to love and be with the other parent.**
- **Be completely responsible** for the children's emotional and physical health, safety, and conduct when your child is in your care.[1]
- **Learn about the things children need parents to know** (see Chapters 9 and 10). Learn about the danger signals[2] children show, and immediately take action if they appear.
- **Keep children away from your adult issues,** even when they want to be involved. They should not play referee, judge, spy, or pass messages for you, and they definitely should not pick sides or watch or hear your fights.
- **Keep the transfers of children peaceful and organized** so children will be free of stress and feel okay about going with the other parent. Be on time.
- **Try to have your two homes close to your child's school and friends.**
- **Be in frequent contact with your child when you are separated.** Use the phone, texts, emails, Skype, photos, videos, audios. Let them know they are important to you.
- **Enjoy your time with your child.** Childhood passes all too quickly.

You and the Other Parent

- **Be calm, courteous, and diplomatic with the other parent** even when you don't feel like it. Think CCD for short.

Put your child first. Love your child more than you dislike or distrust the other parent

put kids first
1

Be calm, courteous, and diplomatic with the other parent even when you don't feel like it.

- **Do not make plans on the other parent's time** without his or her permission, and don't mix your parenting business with your business as former partners.
- **Uphold each other as parents.** No fair undermining each other's authority or importance in your child's life.
- **Respect boundaries between your homes and your personal lives.** Keep your personal lives private unless they affect the children and don't pry into the other's private life.
- **Confide in only one or two of your closest friends and your health or legal professional.** Be sure these people will keep your confidences and not spread gossip about you or against the other parent. Try to avoid confiding in mutual friends.
- **Keep each other updated** on the essentials about your child, schooling, and any major problems (see Chapter 6 on Communications). At the least, email an update to the other parent in a brief paragraph the day before the child goes there.
- **Use specific business-like ways for communicating, handling meetings, and solving problems** so you can side-step the "divorce handcuffs" of hard feelings (see Chapters 4 through 7).
- **Have a solid Parenting Plan and legal agreement**, follow them, and also follow all court orders (see Chapter 11).
- **Make decisions and work out disagreements in a peaceful way.** See a mediator or counselor for the most difficult issues.
- **If you have a new love in your life**, tell the other parent well before you introduce the children to this new person, and tell the other parent what, if any, involvement or authority the new partner will have in the care of the children.[3]
- **If you have a new partner**, discuss these Basic CoParenting Guidelines with them, and ask for his or her cooperation and support as you implement them with your coparent.
- **If you and the other parent disagree on major issues** for longer than two weeks, see a mediator or a coparenting counselor.
- **Expect your close relatives to act CCD with the other parent** especially when the children are present.
- **Follow these Guidelines even if the other parent does not.**

If it's hard to live up to any of these Guidelines, look at the "Limited CoParenting Guidelines" in the next chapter.

$$\boxed{\textbf{TIPS}}$$

FOR USING THE BASIC COPARENTING GUIDELINES

■ Take it one step at a time

The Basic CoParenting Guidelines are a lot to think about all at once, especially if you are just now in the process of separation. If you are feeling discouraged, don't feel guilty. We are all human. If you read the rest of this *Toolkit*, there should be some things you can find that can encourage you and your efforts. This book is here to support you.

■ CoParenting means giving up total control

When you were with your spouse or partner, you were both completely responsible for your child at all times. But with coparenting, you turn over a lot of that responsibility to the other parent when your child is with him or her. Don't interfere with their time together unless you believe your child is at risk. When you lived together you may have made plans for your child independently, but now you can't make plans for your child on the other parent's time. That time no longer belongs to you. It can feel very strange. For some parents, it can be heartbreaking to watch your children leave you for their time with the other parent. As painful as this might be, when you have a court order or legal Parenting Plan that says what days and nights the children are with you and when they are with the other parent, it is the law, and you are expected to follow it.

■ Keep your children out of the middle

Even though you and the other parent may have some issues between you, you need to protect your children from getting involved in your "stuff." These problems belong to you, the adults, not the kids. This includes older children, too. It's far too easy for children to play referee, judge, take sides, become our confidants, or tell tales. This doesn't help them or you. Your child should see and hear you and others being respectful and courteous with the other parent. Sure, you may want to be sarcastic, shout, or slam the door, but it's a no-win situation for anyone if you do

If you have already put most of the Basic CoParenting Guidelines into practice, congratulations!

well done

it. Finally, try to make it easy for your child to feel free about loving and missing the other parent. When parents don't like or trust each other, or one parent feels deeply wounded, children can't help but pick that up. Still, it's not our child's burden. They don't have the same problem with the other parent that we have. Be sure to read Chapter 7 about the "miserable middle."

■ Be Calm, Courteous, and Diplomatic, "CCD"

Easy to do? Often not. Sometimes impossible. There's often a gap between what we think we should do, and what actually happens. All that controlled behavior can feel out of reach. Well, join the club. You have lots of company. Just do the best you can and try to stay open to new information that can help you be "CCD." It's doable. It just takes time and your attention. Chapters 4 through 6 have many strategies and tips for how to learn how to do this, and you can develop it little by little. This is not just good basic coparenting, but it can also help you let go of some of the old baggage from your former relationship and avoid the quicksand of the cold (or hot) war between you.

You love your child. It can help to remind yourself that you love your child more than you dislike or distrust the other parent. This reminder can make it easier to be "CCD" and to put your child first.

■ CoParenting roadsigns for communication

One of the biggest jobs for parents is to put together a system for how to communicate and work together as a team. If you read *Chapter 6: Try These Tools to Side-Step Communication Potholes,* you might save yourself some time and frustration. For example, plan to regularly email an update to the other parent in a brief paragraph the day before your child changes homes. Of course, keep each other up to date in between on what's important at school, your child's health and moods, friends, and activities. But try not to forget that regular update. The other parent wants to know what's going on, and when you give that update, it can be a step toward more trust and less stress. Tip: If giving the other parent simple information about your child causes problems between you, it's time to see a coparent counselor to iron this out.

■ Hard feelings and misunderstandings

When it comes to hard feelings and major misunderstandings, you can try a series of tools. First, read and re-read *Chapter 4: Speed Healing by Managing Hurt and Hard Feelings 5: Use Business Guidelines for Relating to the Other Parent,* and start using some of those tips and guides. Second, if things are really stressful, then shift lanes and start using the "Limited CoParenting Guidelines" to help you find ways to meet the Basic CoParenting Guidelines. They are described in the next chapter.

Try to work out disagreements or problems in a relatively peaceful way. This can be an uphill climb. Use Chapter 6 and Chapter 8 for strategies and tips to make this easier for you. If you still get stuck, talk to a family mediator or coparenting counselor. If you are beginning the process of divorce, you also might want to explore the Collaborative Divorce process.

■ The new love in your life

As wonderful as this new love in your life is for you, when it comes to the kids and the other parent—well, maybe not so much. This is a major period of adjustment for them as well as for you. Respectfully advise the other parent well before you introduce the children to this new person. If you and a new partner are going to live together, tell the other parent before the move, and especially what, if any, authority or responsibility the new partner will have for the care of the children. Show the Basic CoParenting Guidelines to your new partner and ask for his or her cooperation and support.

■ Enlist friends and family

If any family members have issues with the other parent, be clear that you want them to be respectful and courteous to him or her particularly when the children are present. If you show these Guidelines to family members and close friends, hopefully they can better appreciate what coparenting needs to work well and ways they can help. Coparents can use all the support they can get.

Finally, protect your confidential information. Try to only confide in a close friend or two or a trusted family member. Please choose people who can keep a secret and not pass on this sensitive and highly private information—especially about your former mate. This is your child's other parent and you probably have mutual friends. Negative gossip can deeply hurt your child. Besides, it has a very long shelf life.

• •

Roberto said after reading this list, "If I had done all that when I was married, I might not be divorced today." Maybe yes, but maybe no. Now, however, he has another chance to give his children a good example of how adults can step up and work together when it's for a high purpose, such as their love and commitment to their children.

• •

HOW COPARENTING GUIDELINES
CAN HELP AVOID HASSLES

Cody and Laura have a temporary time schedule issued by the court that gives each of them specific days with their children. They haven't read the Basic CoParenting Guidelines yet. As a result, Cody makes plans for one of their daughters to attend a friend's birthday party on Laura's time without telling her or getting her permission. But it's Laura's parent time, and she becomes angry—something that seems to happen frequently when it comes to Cody. Cody didn't check with her first, and now she'll be the bad guy in the family if she tells her daughter she can't go to the party. Laura says Cody doesn't respect her rights. Cody thinks that the birthday party invitation came during his time with their daughter and that he should make that decision. The parents argue in front of their children. Laura threatens to call her lawyer. Their daughter wanted to go to the party, but now feels she's to blame for her parents' argument. It becomes a domino effect of unintended consequences. It's a mess.

One of the Basic Guidelines reads, *"Do not make plans on the other parent's time without his or her permission."* Oops! If Cody had known, he could have sent Laura a text describing the invitation because he realizes he isn't supposed to make that decision. And he could have told his daughter that she needed to clear this with her Mom first.

Another Basic Guideline reads, *"Be sure your child sees and hears you and others being respectful and courteous with the other parent and*

Monika and Roberto

Monika and Roberto believe their own brand of the Basic CoParenting Guidelines is working well. They respect each other as parents, are naturally "CCD," and do put the children first. But after reading the Guidelines, Monika realizes she has not yet talked to Roberto about her boyfriend Vern and the children. She and Roberto meet for coffee. She assures Roberto that Vern does not stay overnight when the children are there and that he does not discipline them. Roberto wants Monika to support him as the children's father and that he is and always will be the Dad. He wants to meet Vern soon, even if it's just for a few minutes. Roberto asks Monika to tell him if she does get engaged or lives with Vern. She agrees to let him know before she tells the children. They both feel better.

---

the other parent's partner." If Laura had realized how very important this guideline was to basic coparenting, she might have thought twice about letting her temper get the best of her before she raised her voice, was sarcastic, and let the argument develop in front of the kids.

> **Question:** Laura asked, "I know these Basic Guidelines would be good to follow, but I have to be realistic. Even though we say we are both committed to coparenting, we aren't following a lot of the Guidelines about how we treat each other. So what are our next steps?"
>
> **Answer:** The way you and Cody work together is not expected to be perfect, but it needs to be the best possible arrangement you can put together for now. First, use as many of the "Limited CoParenting Guidelines" in the next chapter as you can. These Guidelines are the add-ons for meeting the Basic Guidelines. These could give you some distance from one another and help reduce your number of arguments.
>
> You'll find a series of tools on how to put the Limited Guidelines and the Basic Guidelines into action starting with *Chapter 3: Use Your Strengths and Set Your Course.* Then read the next three chapters on managing hard feelings, using business guidelines to communicate, and avoiding the miserable middle. These chapters can all work together for you. Since you are working with a mediator for your divorce settlement, also look at Chapter 11 on Parenting Plans and Chapter 12 on Schedules.

Guidelines Are Important

When each parent understands the Basic Coparenting rules, they can know when they are on the right road to healthy coparenting and when they are not. The next chapter talks about the other lanes on the CoParenting Highway for times when things go really well (flexible coparenting) and when hard feelings rule the road (limited coparenting).

Coparenting can take many forms and people develop their own style, but there are still basic expectations for what's okay and what's not.

NOTES FOR CHAPTER 1

1. Chapter 10 in *Mom's House, Dad's House* is a good resource on parenting responsibility (pp. 133–154).

2. *Mom's House, Dad's House*, p. 149, has a Table of Danger Signals given by children when they are in distress.

3. When parents date, children are strongly affected. See *Mom's House, Dad's House for KIDS*, pp. 114–120, for more information, and *Mom's House, Dad's House*, pp. 358–359, for suggested guidelines on if, when, and how to introduce a new love into the children's lives.

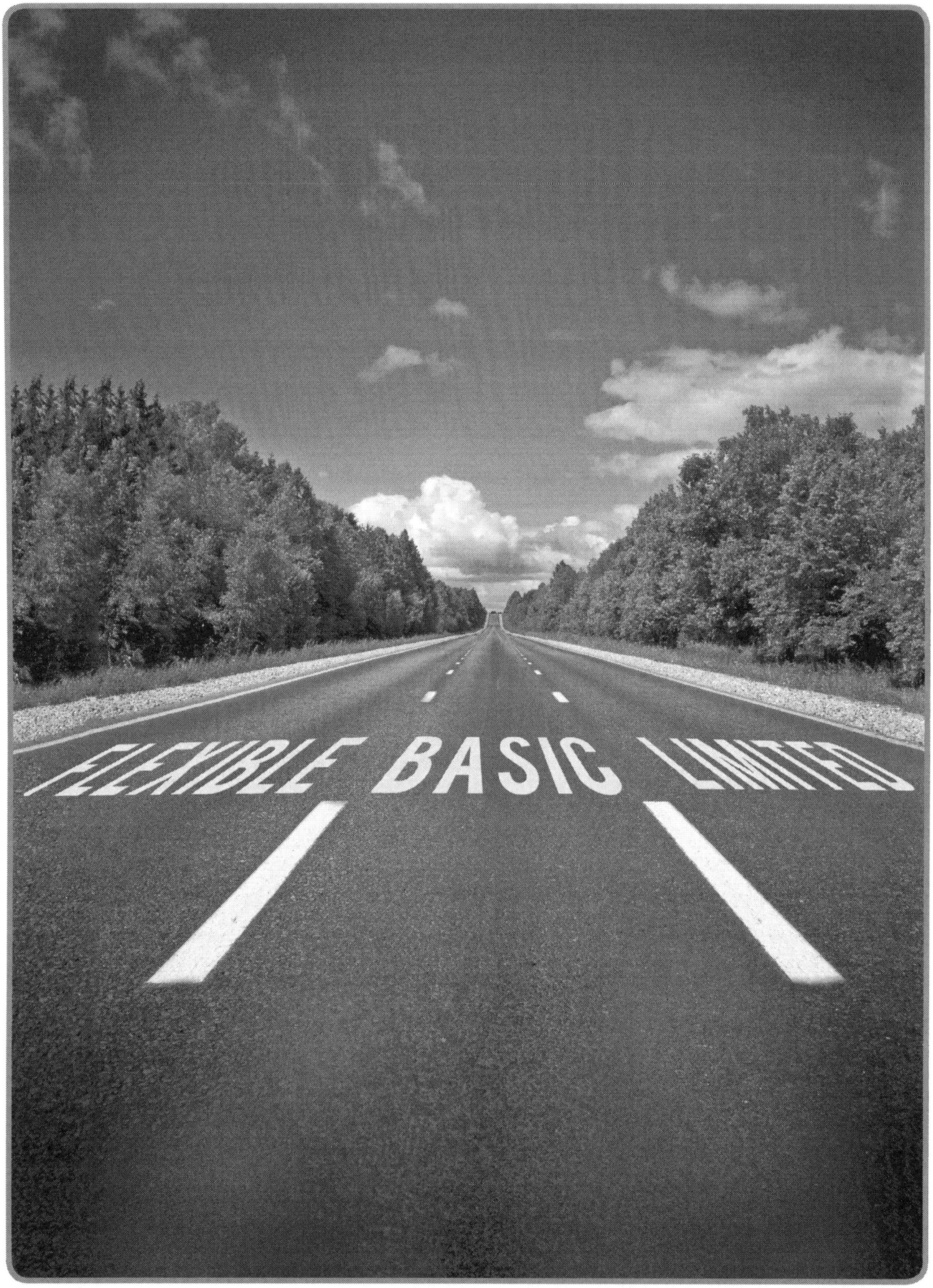
FLEXIBLE BASIC LIMITED

CHAPTER
2

Switch Lanes for More Flexible or More Limited CoParenting

Flexible CoParenting—The Left Lane
Flexible Guidelines for CoParenting
Limited CoParenting—The Right Lane
Limited Guidelines for CoParenting
Dangers of Long-Term Limited CoParenting
Your Own Combination of CoParenting Guidelines

Chapter 1 was all about the Basic CoParenting Guidelines—the big center lane for parents on the CoParenting Highway and the guidelines all coparents should follow. This chapter is about the other two "lanes." Every family has its own personality. Some parents may find the Basic CoParenting Guidelines easy. Others will find them a major challenge. With these two additional lanes in the CoParenting Highway, you have more ways for meeting the basics. Picture them this way:

Left Lane: Flexible CoParenting Guidelines for when things go really well

Right Lane: Limited CoParenting Guidelines for when hard feelings rule

When things go well, enjoy flexible coparenting.

FLEXIBLE COPARENTING—THE LEFT LANE

Active Teamwork

Flexible CoParenting is a blessed relief! It is active teamwork! It builds on the Basic Guidelines and adds flexibility, tolerance, and more mutual support. It's more responsive and parents trust that each parent is putting the child's needs first.

More Efficiency and Less Stress

Flexible coparenting is like overdrive in a car. Doing things for the children seems to take less effort when you are not spending energy on arguments or negative emotions. Flexible Guidelines include natural add-ons for times when people can cover some or most of the basics fairly well and become more flexible with their schedule, communication, and how they team up as parents. Coparents who spend a lot of time in this lane are typically a strong team.

  Don't think you have to do everything in this list. Just pick and choose what feels right to you. Add your own version to what's "flexible." The goal is create your own ways to keep coparenting on track, supporting your kids, and getting on with your life.

well done

FLEXIBLE GUIDELINES

FOR COPARENTING

Teamwork and Mutual Support

- Find a separation and divorce group for your child to attend so he or she can be with other kids having similar experiences.
- Consider taking a parenting class together with your coparent.
- Actively support your child's schooling, homework, and activities as a team, not just as separate parents. Attend teacher conferences together.
- Have House and Safety Rules that are the same in each home, especially for discipline, and carry these over from one home to the next. Also try to have the same rules for homework, bedtime, curfews, activities, time with friends, communications, and use of the family car.
- When a serious discipline or other situation arises, first talk about this together privately, decide on what to do and say, and then talk to the child or children together.
- Consider your individual parenting styles (look at Chapters 9 and 10). If you have widely different styles, consult with a counselor to iron out the key issues.

- Manage to attend as many as you can of your child's school events and activities together. Behave so your child can take pride in you both.
- Coordinate how you will volunteer at school and for afterschool events.
- Make it easy for the children to see all their grandparents, cousins, and friends, including those on the other parent's side.
- Keep a written schedule or calendar for who is where and who does what, and have it accessible to everyone, including the other parent.
- Have your two homes close to your child's school and friends.
- Use a coparenting counselor or mediator before disagreements spiral out of control.
- Go beyond the usual coparenting communications guidelines and keep each other well-informed about your child's moods, dreams, interests, and worries.
- Spend a few hours together with your child to celebrate his or her birthday. Some parents spend a few hours together on major holidays as well.
- When a parent is sick and there is no one to help, offer to take the children, bring the parent to a doctor, or provide other support. Be a good model for your children for how families support each other.
- Switch to some "Limited CoParenting Guidelines" where and when you need to.

TIPS

FOR FLEXIBLE COPARENTING

■ **Few coparents can be flexible with all things.**

Perhaps parents are flexible around family get-togethers, supporting the children's schooling and activities, or they have the same house rules. But, even flexible parents can find solving particular problems too exhausting to do on their own. They want to save time, energy, and good will so they bring in a neutral third party like a mediator or a coparenting counselor. These things happen. It doesn't mean that the rest of the coparenting relationship is falling apart. Not at all. Instead it means that flexible parents don't want to beat an argument to death and still not solve the problem.

■ Flexible coparenting is not the same as being "best friends."

Instead, it is a strong parenting partnership. Parents are friendly and CCD, but they are not "friends" in the usual sense. They don't share a lot of personal information unless it affects the children. There is a good reason for this. Chapters 4 and 5 explain this further. However, even though parents aren't best friends, they can and do support each other with emergencies and special needs.

■ If you get off track.

There is a "second wave" of emotional boobytraps that can upset any coparenting partnership, even a flexible coparenting one.[1] For example, the other parent gets married, or gets a new partner, or there's a new baby, a new job. Perhaps a teenager decides to live with the other parent, or a parent moves away. These events can stir up emotions, and the easy give and take the parents once enjoyed gets unsettled and even undermined. People often have to readjust their schedules, their expectations, and their responsibilities. Sometimes, there's a roadblock. Perhaps a new partner thinks the coparenting relationship is unnatural or proof that there is still a romantic possibility. On the other hand, a parent may worry that the new partner will take his or her place with the children—a frightening thought! Be sure any new partner reads and gets on board with the Basic CoParenting Guidelines and takes a look at the other two sets of CoParenting Guidelines as well.

■ It pays to be a flexible team.

When you see coparents acting as a team, you can believe that they have put out a lot of effort to get to a place where they can put the children first, value each other's strengths as parents, work out their differences, and honor their agreements. Their reward is two homes where children have the opportunity to be the best that they can be and the parents themselves are able to get on with their lives without dragging along the unhealthy baggage of the past.

Monika and Robert

Monika and Roberto have a relatively low stress and flexible relationship. They have the same routines for the children at their homes, and if Sam or Nell wants to stay longer with a parent, the other parent usually consents. They also switch days or times for a special event or to spend time with relatives and friends. They give one birthday party for each child where they both attend with their families. When 8-year-old Sam got into fights at school, both parents went together to talk to teachers where they developed a plan for Sam. Recently, when Monika was very ill with the flu, the children stayed with Roberto and they brought her food and picked up her prescriptions. The children knew their mother was well cared for and they didn't need to worry.

LIMITED COPARENTING—THE RIGHT LANE

Limited CoParenting Has Extra Help for Meeting the Basic Guidelines

When people are burdened and stressed with all the issues and emotions that come along with separation and divorce, they may not want to have anything to do with the other parent—at all. They may want to coparent, but some or many of the Basic CoParenting Guidelines seem way out of range. Here's where Limited CoParenting Guidelines can help. These Guidelines are in the "extra help" right lane where you can still be active parents but there's less going on as coparents—sometimes a lot less. The Limited CoParenting Guidelines aren't a free pass from the Basic Guidelines. Instead they let you slow down and regroup, so you can eventually meet the Basic Guidelines.

Limited CoParenting Guidelines are useful when you come to the rougher spots in the road such as hard feelings, arguments, not following agreements, or communications issues. A Limited CoParenting pattern is a close relative of something often called "parallel parenting."[2] When limited coparenting works well, it can give you both some distance and perspective, help things cool down,[3] and help you get back in control.

When hard feelings rule, try limited coparenting.

Limited CoParenting Can Help Newly Separated Parents

Parents often seem to use a version of limited coparenting during those months after separation when they are not at their best and get caught in that tangled nest of distrust, hurt, frustration, or anger. In some ways, these Guidelines are like a "time-out" for grownups. As you will see later in this chapter, Limited CoParenting can work for a while. However, it should be a short-term solution, because it carries many risks for children if it goes on too long.

LIMITED GUIDELINES

FOR COPARENTING

Limited CoParenting Guidelines do not replace the Basic CoParenting Guidelines. Instead they are designed to help you eventually meet the Basic Guidelines.

Extra Help for Meeting the Basics

- Think "separate but equal" parenting. You are parenting from two different worlds but your child needs consistency. Try to have as many of the same House and Safety Rules as possible. This is very important.
- Follow your Parenting Plan, court order, and agreements to the letter. There is no wiggle room here.
- Have a Parenting Plan that is as specific and detailed as possible with sections on what will happen if an agreement is not followed.
- Find a fair way to divide up responsibilities and decisions for activities and certain responsibilities for your child. If you try to share them while you are dealing with short tempers or misunderstandings, there may be even more conflict. Put together a "Who Does What List" (Chapter 11). If you can't do this together, use a mediator for a session or two.
- Use email, texts, and tweets. Face-to-face meetings, phone conversations, and voicemail messages may not be the best choice right now. Use the Email Etiquette Guidelines in Chapter 6.
- You must still communicate with the other parent about your child, but now put a limit on how often. Make it short and courteous. Send a weekly update, but limit any other communications to one or two topics at a time.

- Keep your conversations about the children separate from those about finances or the divorce.

- Be extra clear about the children's schedule for medications, homework, activities, and medical concerns.

- Try using a folder that goes back and forth with your child for anything that comes to you about school or an activity. Make your own copy of what's in that folder for your own separate file.

- Each of you should obtain your own private copies of the school and "outside school" activity calendars and other information such as camps unless you have agreed otherwise. If you have the total responsibility for an activity, be sure the other parent is on the emergency list and has a schedule for that activity.

- Until you can talk about your child's moods, friends, and fears without slipping into negative or "passive aggressive"[4] behavior, only communicate about these if there is a problem.

- Protect your child from hearing or watching your conflicts. Please behave respectfully with one another in your child's presence.

- When you need to be in the same place at the same time, acknowledge each other cordially or with a friendly wave. If you can't be in the same room or at an activity together, then find a way so you don't run into each other.

- Your limited coparenting period should be a time for learning how to manage your hard feelings, fine tune your communications, and find different strategies for solving problems. It's best if you use this time to invest in a better coparenting arrangement for the future rather than allow it to become a long-term standoff.

$\boxed{\textsf{TIPS}}$

FOR LIMITED COPARENTING

■ Be super strict about keeping your child from your conflicts

The Basic CoParenting Guidelines say to keep your children away from your adult issues. An adult's negatively charged emotions or disrespectful behavior can be far too intense for kids to manage. Pay special attention to any times when your children might watch or listen to your arguments or know too much about your problems with one another. For example, when parents argue or are disrespectful, children often feel they either have to take a side, jump in and fix something, feel responsible for your problems, or pass messages for you. If this is happening, find a way to stop it. Chapters 4 through 8 have many tools to try for getting along with the other parent and using communications in a positive way.

As strange as it may sound, pay attention to how easy it is for a child to access your personal papers, phone voicemails, or emails. Even when you think these papers are secure, when parents are at a high level of conflict, some children feel the need to snoop, and unfortunately some parents actually ask them to do so. Chapter 7 on the Miserable Middle has tips and strategies specially designed for keeping your child protected.

■ Your child must always see and hear you being respectful with the other parent and his or her partner

This applies to all forms of parenting and coparenting, but it is critical when you and the other parent are in this "limited coparenting" situation. Disrespect, sarcasm, or contempt is toxic for your child. This includes your phone or other conversations children may overhear (not just with the other parent). No exceptions.

■ Put on a good face in public

Make it easy for your child. If you are at an activity together with your child and the other parent is there, perhaps with his or her partner, you and your partner must be calm, courteous, and diplomatic. Even if they are not. There is no room for attitude, dirty looks, snide remarks, or pretending the other person isn't there. It's humiliating and upsetting for a child to have parents act this way, especially in public. Please protect them from this. You don't have to sit together, but do acknowledge each other courteously. This can put your child and others there at ease. If you can't be in the same schoolroom for School Open House or at a child's activity like a Holiday Pageant, divide the time so you don't overlap, or divide the events you attend.

■ Follow your court orders and Parenting Plans exactly

When you and the other parent have problems, it can take more effort to follow court orders and Parenting Plans. But this is exactly the time when you must follow them to the letter. When anger or resentment is very high, don't even think about asking for a change in the schedule or routine.

■ Have a detailed Parenting Plan

When conflict is high and trust is low, have your Parenting Plan be as specific and detailed as possible. It should also have defaults and consequences if an agreement is not followed. Further, if your Plan says you are to discuss and share decision making, seriously consider dividing these decisions and their responsibilities between each of you instead of having to discuss or haggle over every single decision together every time. If you are trapped in a swamp of distrust, negative emotions, or misunderstandings, go to Chapter 11 on Parenting Plans, and make out your own "Who Does What" list. If you can't make out this list within two or three weeks, see a mediator or coparenting counseling specialist to finish this up. Then you can use the completed list to stay out of each other's hair. Try not to drag out your disagreements. It's a no-win situation.

■ Put a limit on your contacts with your coparent, and make them brief

When contact easily develops into trouble, limit your contacts to what's absolutely necessary. Face-to-face meetings, phone conversations, and voicemail messages may not be wise. Instead use email, texts, and tweets and be brief and courteous. Use the Email Etiquette Guidelines in Chapter 6. The longer people talk or write, the greater the potential for losing emotional control.

The longer people talk or write, the greater the potential for losing emotional control.

■ Tell each other the important things about your child's life

Keep each other updated on the essentials, especially illness, medications, homework, and activities. Kids feel safer when both parents are on the same page. As Chapter 6 describes in more detail, do a brief email report—a short paragraph—on what your child did when he or she was with you and email it the day before the transition to the other parent. If older children are in regular phone or email contact with the other parent, this may not seem as important, but it's still a good idea. Children's interpretations of events often differ from their parents'.

■ The homework and activities challenge

Even when parents never separate, keeping homework, class require-ments, and outside activities straight is a never-ending task. Try using a homework folder or school folder for anything that comes to you about school or an activity. This master folder goes back and forth with your child. Please make a copy of every new paper that your child brings home or that you obtain on your own. Put the originals in that master folder and send it to the other parent with your child and keep a copy of everything for yourself. Both of you need to do this. Also notice that the Limited Coparenting Guidelines recommend that each of you separately obtain the calendars and other information about other activities and that you don't count on the other parent to get these for you.

■ The House and Safety Rules solution

Agree on as many common House and Safety Rules as possible for both your homes. This consistency is a key ingredient to a child's sense of continuity and security. If this is difficult to create together, get help from a mediator. If you have different parenting styles, be sure to read Chapters 9 and 10 and then try to construct or revise your house and safety rules.

■ Learn how to get along—somehow

When parents find it difficult, even impossible, to communicate and get along, it's usually because of harsh feelings, distrust, and bad experiences with one another. Even if you do a good job of protecting your child from these feelings, children can still sense them and it's toxic for them.

Use Chapters 4 through 8 to help you manage your relationship with the other parent. Try these time-tested tools and see if, after you put them into practice, they make a positive difference in your life. You might save yourself time and frustration if you can also work with a counselor, minister, or therapist who is trained to work with families in these situations.

No matter what the issues are between you and the other parent, you do not have an issue with your child. The time that you spend with your child should be all about your child.

■ Be good to yourself

Finally, be good to yourself! There are ways to neutralize these feelings over time. So, target that "emotional baggage" that might still be hanging around from the old relationship.

Cody and Laura

Cody and Laura went over the Limited CoParenting Guidelines. The first thing they finally agreed to do was to only communicate by email and texts and to be sure they didn't mix talking about the children with talk about their legal divorce and property. This was a relief. The second thing they did was to talk with their mediator about how to make their Parenting Plan more specific. Then, Cody asked Laura to send him weekly updates on what each of the children was doing, but Laura hasn't done this as yet. As for getting along, Laura secretly feels that Cody's affair is to blame for the family's problems while Cody feels that Laura is clueless about how difficult it was for him and the children to live with her personality. These parents have a lot to think about. The information in the next six chapters offers them support and tools. How will they use them?

Question: When we were together, we didn't treat each other calmly, courteously, or diplomatically. Why should I start now?"

Answer: It's never too late to help your children and free yourself from the past. The way you related in marriage didn't work, and that old way probably won't work in coparenting, either. So remember the motto: **The Children's Needs Come First.** Try using some of the tools in this book to move forward.

Question: It looks like we're headed into a messy divorce about finances and the sale of the house. We used to work together as parents

My marriage didn't work, but I am committed to doing my very best as a parent and coparent now.

—A coparenting Dad

When parents use a neutral third party, they can often begin to really hear what the other person is saying instead of automatically tuning them out.

when we were married. Now, I can follow some of the Basic Guidelines, but others seem impossible. She won't talk to me at all. Is coparenting a lost cause?

Answer: No. Don't give up yet. You once worked together well, and that is a good sign. You have three major efforts: 1) to try to find a way to coparent successfully; 2) to be as good a parent as you can be; 3) to emerge from your divorce with a relatively fair distribution of assets and liabilities and as little acrimony as possible. People's emotions and reactions to the divorce process can easily interfere with their ability to talk reasonably about the children. If you haven't already done so, consider investigating different ways to come to an agreement outside of court. You might look into the Collaborative Law approach,[5] family mediation,[6] a coparent counselor, or speak to a counselor at your place of worship.

If your emotions get in the way of coparenting, you might also think about including mandatory coparent counseling as part of your temporary or final court order. When parents use a neutral third party, they can often begin to really hear what the other person is saying instead of automatically tuning them out. Perhaps here is where your desire to be an active parent will get a fair hearing and where you can listen to the concerns of the other parent as well. In any case, talk to an attorney about your legal options.

Keep in mind that no matter what path you take to get through the legal divorce, it's what you yourself bring to your interactions with the other parent that are important. Become as informed as possible.

DANGERS OF LONG-TERM LIMITED COPARENTING

For many reasons, when limited coparenting goes on too long, there can be significant risks for your child. The damage to children from ongoing conflict is well-documented in research. Even more worrisome is that children's problems are often hidden from view and manifest later.

Here are just a few of the dangers and risks.

1. The child may find the differences between the two homes exhausting, frustrating, or confusing. He or she is powerless to get changes for the better and may suffer by becoming withdrawn, depressed, anxious, oppositional, manipulative, or combative.
2. Parents who avoid discussions about their child usually do not share with each other enough of the right information about their children's moods, fears, and dreams. The child is deprived of a parent team who connects with him or her on a deeper level.
3. If one or both parents continue their open conflict, the child may end up in the middle of the parents' battles and may be asked to choose sides or protect one parent. The child may do so, not because who they choose is the most deserving, but because their inner pain is so great they feel they must align with someone just to emotionally survive.
4. If conflict and hostility between parents continue over time, a child may seem to "adjust," but to do so they may need to become emotionally detached. This can seriously undermine a child's ability to feel for others, stand up for themselves, receive affection, or make close relationships.
5. Children are keenly aware when their parents actively do not like or accept each other. A child may try to fix the problem, feel responsible for their parents' happiness, or take responsibility for causing the problems. A child often tells the parent what he or she thinks the parent needs to hear.
6. A child learns by watching others, especially their parents. What are their parents teaching them about how people should treat one another?

   What if limited coparenting doesn't work? What if one or both parents are irresponsible or disrespectful? Or continues to put a child in the middle? Even after parents try their best and the situation continues

Long-term limited coparenting is asking the children to live with their parents' differences and distrust while trying somehow to please them both. This is very hard for mature adults to do. It's a lot to ask of a child.

CAUTION

If parents and stepparents or other family members fuel suspicion and resentments, the healing process can go off track. Then, the risks to children grow even more serious. Something must be done. Seek professional help. Your child comes first.

to be unhealthy, then what? One option is to do nothing and hope things get better on their own and soon. A safer option is to find an experienced coparenting counselor to help you decide if coparenting is going to work for everyone. Ideally, both of you work with the counselor, but if the other parent refuses, then get some advice yourself on how to proceed. When information comes from a neutral third party, it can sometimes help parents turn things around. It often helps parents to attend intensive 3–6-week parent education classes such as Kids Turn. Seminars and classes such as these usually offer information and research about the effects of divorce on children—especially where there is high conflict—and what parents can do. In *Appendix 9, When You Have Done All You Can Do*, there are suggestions for next steps.

The secret to using Limited CoParenting Guidelines. The secret to success is to use your time with limited coparenting to gradually do what will help you move toward more teamwork and mutual respect so you can meet all of the Basic CoParenting Guidelines.

YOUR OWN COMBINATION OF COPARENTING GUIDELINES

Shift Lanes When Needed or Possible!

You can shift between the three lanes and make up your own combination of Guidelines. This combination will probably change as the children grow older and your needs as parents change. Many parents stick to the Basic Guidelines for most things and use the Limited Guidelines for certain issues. They also appreciate the freedom of the Flexible style. You may never get to a fully flexible arrangement, but that's not the goal. The goal is to find your own coparenting arrangement that works for you and your children, and that meets the Basic Guidelines as much as is possible.

NOTES FOR CHAPTER 2

1. See p. 65 of *Mom's House, Dad's House* for a description of the First and Second Waves of ending relationships.

2. The term *Parallel Parenting* was first presented by the author at the Association of Family and Conciliation Courts International Conference (Boston, May 1986), quoted in a CA Appellate Court decision (*California Family Law Monthly*, 1989, 6:45–56), and later published in "Mediation, Joint Custody and Legal Agreements: A Time to Review, Revise and Refine," *Family and Conciliation Courts Review*, 1989, 27:47–55. It is also noted in the second edition of *Mom's House, Dad's House*, p. 116

(1997), and has been an ongoing subject in the author's trainings and workshops for professionals.

3. In this *Toolkit*, dealing with difficulties with the other parent has been enlarged and expanded from *Mom's House, Dad's House*.

4. Passive-aggressive behavior is often defined as being manipulative, secretive, withholding or "stonewalling," stockpiling resentments, spreading rumors, silent treatment, or pretending support or agreement but not following through.

5. To learn more, see website for the International Academy of Collaborative Professionals, http://www.collaborativepractice.com/.

6. To learn more about family mediation, go to Chapter 15, pp. 233–243, in *Mom's House, Dad's House*. To find a mediator, ask your attorney or mental health professional for a referral. You may also search at http://www.mediate.com/mediator/search.cfm. This site also offers referrals for Parenting Coordinators.

CHAPTER
3

Use Your Strengths and
Set Your Course

Use Your Strengths
Quiz: What Are Your Strengths?
What Do You Want for Your Child?
Quiz: What Worries You?
Wakeup Calls

USE YOUR STRENGTHS

Successful coparents shine a light on strengths, acknowledge them, and protect them. This is a very important tool for helping them meet the Basic CoParenting Guidelines. In the Introduction to this book, you answered some questions about your commitment to coparenting, your child's need for the other parent in his or her life, and the other parent's commitment to parenting and coparenting. Your "Yes" answers there are your most important strengths. Commitment is the glue that holds things together when coparenting gets shaky. Once you have the foundation of basic commitment, there's a lot more good stuff that follows.

You have strengths, and so does the other parent. These may be hidden right now under the rush of daily life or perhaps painful experiences, but they are there. The Quiz that follows is a way to remind yourself of your own strengths and the strengths of the other parent. Once these strengths are in the spotlight, the next step is to find ways to acknowledge them.

Commitment is the glue that holds things together when coparenting gets shaky.

QUIZ

WHAT ARE YOUR STRENGTHS?

Answer these questions as a parent not as a former partner.

1 **You as a parent: What strengths do you particularly like in yourself?** Circle any you appreciate. Then add your own.

Dependable, trustworthy, responsive, warm, affectionate, kind, sympathetic, gentle, strong, loving, predictable, attentive, committed, fun, detail-oriented, consistent, honest, helpful, reliable, courageous, sense of humor, playful, protective, patient, coaches, teaches life skills, family-oriented, well-grounded, stable, secure, curious, respectful, loyal, creative, practical, thinker, down-to-earth, optimistic, high integrity, persistent, resilient, engaged, etc.

Write in more_____

2 **The other parent as a parent: What strengths do you particularly appreciate?** Circle any you appreciate. Then add your own.

Dependable, trustworthy, responsive, warm, affectionate, kind, sympathetic, gentle, strong, loving, predictable, attentive, committed, fun, detail-oriented, consistent, honest, helpful, reliable, courageous, sense of humor, playful, protective, patient, coaches, teaches life skills, family-oriented, well-grounded, stable, secure, curious, respectful, loyal, creative, practical, thinker, down-to-earth, optimistic, high integrity, persistent, resilient, engaged, etc.

Write in more_____

Give credit where credit is due.

Strength Boosters

1. **Congratulate yourself on your strengths.** Yes, do it. Separation and divorce have a way of draining our self-confidence, and it's important to remind yourself about what you do right. Your strengths are a gift to your children, to yourself, and to others. Even if you have been parenting for many years, take a little time to reflect and appreciate them.

2. **Look at the strengths you identified for the other parent.**

    ☐ Then, write these out in **your private notebook**.

    ☐ Put a brief example next to each strength that describes how that strength benefits the kids.

3. **Prepare to acknowledge and support the other parent's strengths,** *even if you are upset or distrustful of the other parent.*

    ☐ Jot down some ideas on how you can say or write something to the other parent that shows you acknowledge and appreciate how his or her strengths help the children develop and grow. Try not to skip the writing part. When we write things down, our brain connects with the information in a way that can make it easier for you to use the information and build on it.

    ☐ Write out a sample sentence or two that you think you might say to the other parent when you find an opportunity.

    ☐ Write out a sample sentence or two that you think you might say to your child about the other parent's strength when the timing seems right.

    ☐ See the section in Chapter 6, "Acknowledge the Other Parent's Strengths" for examples.

When we write things down, our brain connects with the information in a way that can make it easier for us to use the information and build on it.

Tip: If you have trouble thinking about the other parent's strengths, read Chapter 4, and then come back to this question.

Some Ways to Appreciate a Strength

Cody listed five different strengths for Laura as a mother and Laura listed four strengths for Cody, even though Laura said that it was a challenge for her to even come up with those four. Both wrote down the strengths in their personal notebooks with examples. Cody wrote that he thought Laura was consistent, lively, creative, protective, and fun. One of his examples was: "Laura seems to find a way to make homework more fun without overdoing it." His sample sentence was something he said to the children a week or so later when the twins were talking to him about their homework. "You are lucky kids. Your mother is especially talented at making homework more interesting. I wish I had that when I was your age."

Laura wrote in her notebook that Cody was protective, calm, intelligent, and practical. For "protective", she wrote: "I always know the children are safe and taken care of when they are with him." A month later, when the children were going on a camping trip with Cody, Laura was able to tell him, "I know that the children are always safe when they are with you."

WHAT DO YOU WANT FOR YOUR CHILD?

It's human nature to do better when we have a destination or a goal to work toward. This is one of the main secrets for success. Think about a simple sentence that expresses what you want to give your child as coparents, then write it out. Compose this with the other parent if you can. If not, do it alone. Say this sentence to yourself every day until you believe it. This is an easy way to keep on course, especially if you hit a rough spot in the road with the other parent. Make it simple.[1]

Here are some ideas.

"To always put our children first. This will be our safety test. If we put them first, it will lead us to the best decision."

"To work together peacefully to give our children what they need to live a normal childhood and not be overly stressed or burdened by the separation."

"To give our children the opportunity to know, love, and be raised by parents who are committed to do their best to give them strong life skills, a broad education, and a good start in life."

Goals

Monika and Roberto each wrote out their goals, then emailed them to each other. Their goals were very similar. They combined them into one simple statement, *"We will always think of what our children need first and what is best for them so they can grow up to be happy and have happy families of their own."*

Cody and Laura have so many complications in their family that even though they emailed each other once about their goals, they did not get around to settling on one. As you will see below, they have a lot to think about.

What Worries You?

So far, the spotlight has been on strengths, not just because we can benefit from them but because our strengths are what we can count on to help us with difficult situations. The next page has a list of problems that parents might face. Take inventory. Putting problems into words is one of the first steps in finding solutions or at least something that may make things better. Again, answer these questions for the current situation.

Check the box in the column that has your answer. *Give a separate answer for each child.*

> Take this quiz again in a few months and see what's changed.

✓ What Worries You?

Do You Have Any of These Worries?	YES	SOME	NO
1. The other parent's parenting style	✓	○	○
2. The other parent's attitude toward you	✓	○	○
3. The other parent's values or lifestyle	○	✓	○
4. A stepparent or live-in partner causing problems	○	○	✓
5. Your child's serious health or physical challenges	○	○	✓
6. Your child's emotional health and stability	✓	○	○
7. Your child's academic or learning challenges	○	✓	○
8. Your child's friends or lack of friends	○	✓	○
9. Your child's poor adjustment to two homes	○	○	✓
10. Your child's troublesome behavior and attitude	○	✓	○
11. Your child has taken a side, either with you, or with the other parent against you.	○	○	✓
12. Add your own.	○	○	○

How to Use Your Answers

"No" answers are signs that you think things are going fairly well in that department.

"Some" answers are worth putting on your agenda to talk about.

"Yes" answers are calls for action. You may not be able to solve all these concerns quickly, but please talk about them and what to do next.

Cody and Laura

Cody and Laura email each other their answers. They answered "No" to most questions, but they did have "Some" and "Yes" answers which they shared. Both the parents said that "Yes" they felt disrespected by the other and that they were worried about Matt, their 4-year-old's health. Cody said "Some" about Laura's parenting style. He didn't tell Laura why he worried about her style, but privately he thinks Laura is too rigid and intense with the children. Laura emailed Cody that she also had some concerns about Cody's parenting style but didn't tell him why, either. Privately, Laura thinks that Cody talks a good story, but that even though the children are safe with him he was always too preoccupied to get involved in their activities. She doesn't think this has changed, especially now that he is living with his girlfriend, Hanna. She did tell Cody she didn't like the children staying with him at his girlfriend's house and that she was worried about "troublesome behavior" with their 12-year-old daughter Megan. She has become too thin and is behaving strangely. Laura had not told Cody about this before and Cody had not noticed any changes.

Wakeup Call. Their children need them to pay attention now.

WAKEUP CALLS

When Bad Feelings Hide Other Problems

"Yes" answers are a wakeup call. Cody and Laura had negative feelings about one another that were getting in the way of paying attention to some serious problems with the kids. Now, they are moving quickly to help their children. Laura described Megan's eating and weight loss in more detail to Cody. Cody knew Megan's grades were worse, but he had not noticed an eating problem. Both parents had seen that their 4-year-old's allergies had gotten worse since they had separated, but they hadn't taken him to the pediatrician. These may or may not be very serious problems, but either way the parents need to find out.

Take Action

The parents brought Matt and Megan to their pediatrician. They were shocked to learn that Megan had a potentially serious eating disorder that needed immediate and aggressive intervention and that Matt needed more complicated asthma treatment. The pediatrician was clear that both the children needed a low-stress environment, something they did not have now. The intervention for Megan would include family counseling sessions. The pediatrician strongly recommended that Cody and Laura use these sessions to concentrate on how they could reduce stress all around for the family.

Good Parents Miss Important Signs, Too

Cody and Laura had always thought they knew what was going on with their children, so learning about Matt and especially Megan's very serious health problem was shocking and difficult to believe. They, like so many others, try to be good parents, but the emotions and sheer work involved in separation and divorce have a way of getting children and parents off track. If Cody and Laura didn't have their strengths as parents to call on, they may not have been able to take action on their worries about Megan and Matt. If they weren't committed to coparenting, they might have slipped further into refusing to share information and blaming each other instead of focusing on what was happening to their children. Cody and Laura can use their strengths plus their love for their children to swallow their pride about their relationship and find the road to real solutions for their children (and themselves).

> *Question:* What about situations where one parent sees a problem where a child needs help, but the other parent says the problem doesn't exist and refuses to agree to have it checked out by a professional?
>
> *Answer:* When parents lock horns, it is usually because each of them feels their way is the best way to go, or, sad to say, that one of them can't accept that the other parent might be right. Get the facts first. What exactly does your legal document say about sharing decisionmaking?

Ask your lawyer in what areas you (or the other parent) can move ahead independently of the other parent and where you must both agree. In either case, it can help to read *Chapter 8: Boost Your Skills for Solving Problems* and to look over the example about how parents disentangle their disagreements about a child's needs and move ahead with an action plan.

Question: My children all have different personalities and I'm worried that they won't do well in a two-home situation. What can we do to help them?

Answer: In Chapter 12, you will find an important section on children's temperaments. It is titled, "Your Child's T.L.C." In that same chapter, there are examples of different parents and how they have fashioned schedules for their children based on their child's temperament and personalities.

I have a clearer picture of what we are doing well and where things are risky. Assessing our strengths made sense.
—A coparenting Mom

NOTE FOR CHAPTER 3

1. Pages 114–115 in *Mom's House, Dad's House* has some examples describing parents' hopes and dreams for their children.

CHAPTER

4

Speed Healing by Managing Hurt and Hard Feelings

When Hard Feelings Spill Over into CoParenting
How to Start Building (and Stop Bleeding)
Negative Intimacy—The Dark Side
Quiz: Your Negative Intimacy Inventory
How to Manage Negative Intimacy and Get Back in Control

When parents lived together, they had a life where they shared a bed, the birth of their children, childrearing, celebrations, and worries. When parents separate and go through the process of disentangling their lives, their emotions plus the sheer volume of decisions that need to be made can be overwhelming. In the center of all this is the parents' anguish about their precious children. How can I protect my children? A popular solution is to say, "Share custody so the children will have both parents." But time together is not the full answer.

No matter what your Plan or custody order says about how you share time with your child, it's how you treat one another, how well you work as a parent team, and the quality of your own parenting style that has the bigger influence over your children's development. It also deeply influences how you yourself get on with your life.[1]

So far in this book, we've looked at different tools: CoParenting Guidelines for different coparenting situations, a foundation for coparenting built on your commitment and love for your children, appreciating your strengths as parents and finding ways to use them. In this chapter, you will find some special tools that have been used successfully by scores of parents over many years to help them avoid the quicksand of divorce wars or at least find a way to pull themselves out of them. A happy surprise about these tools is that they can also help with relationships at work as well as ways to neutralize the emotional baggage that might still

Marriage may not be forever, but divorce is.

Find ways to get along, and everything and everyone wins.

be hanging around from the old relationship. Everyone should have the chance to move on with his or her life without dragging that old load.

WHEN HARD FEELINGS SPILL OVER INTO COPARENTING

When Cody and Laura lived together, they usually agreed on big decisions such as choosing a school or a doctor. But now, their hurt and bad feelings have spilled over into their parenting and they are starting to blame one another for their children's problems. Even though they've made a few positive changes, they need to dig deeper in order to build better ways to take charge of themselves and their children's lives again. This chapter and the ones that follow can help.

HOW TO START BUILDING (AND STOP BLEEDING)

How To Use What You Already Know

The first step to getting along with the other parent is to use what you already know about people in general—then **apply it to coparenting** by making some important adjustments. Even though the first information given below seems simple, please don't skip this part, because the tools that come right after it will show you how to make adjustments specifically for coparenting. This could be the single most important thing you can learn from this book.

To begin, look at the Three Levels of Relating graphic. The chart remind us that we act differently in business, with friends, and with intimates. Most people understand that at work people are more reserved and private, but then more relaxed with friends, and the most open and vulnerable with an intimate. But even though this is basic stuff, still take a minute to read all parts of this chart. You will use that information later. Now let's "unpack" how we act depending on where we are and who we are with. **Then, we can use these differences to help construct successful coparenting.**

Business. In business, we may be friendly with our co-workers and our boss, but we're supposed to keep our emotions neutral and the details of our personal life private. Business is business. It's reserved, formal, and there are lots of details and there is a job description. Even if we are upset, we know we have to put a lid on our emotions, stay cool, and be

Three Levels of Relating

Business	**Friendship**	**Intimacy**
Business Rules	Friendship Rules	Private Rules
Neutral Emotions	Some Emotion	Intense Emotions
Formal	More Open	Most Open

careful what we say. We have to stay respectful, courteous, a team player. Even if someone at work is difficult, we're supposed to set that aside and be rational. No drama. "Every day, no matter how tired I am, I have to smile," said one sales representative. "If I want to stay in business, this comes along with the job."

Business usually has a lot of rules, some from laws or licensing requirements, others from policies and procedures. People are expected to keep records, never make assumptions, put things in writing, and be smart about the unwritten rules of being a team player, handling emails, phone calls, and building goodwill for the company.

Friendship. Whether you meet people at work or socially, once people get to know each other better, they may drop some business formalities and become more relaxed together (especially outside of work). People may meet for coffee or share a meal. They might later do social things together, and talk about some of their personal information. As time goes on, acquaintances may feel comfortable revealing more of their experiences and private thoughts. If it goes well, a sense of trust and dependability grows. Over time they may become friends, or even close friends.

Homemakers are business people, too. They manage relationships with doctors, tutors, teachers, maintenance, and service people. They maintain a cordial but still formal relationship with the people with whom they do business. They must make them accountable whether it's returning a bad gallon of milk or insisting that a defective washing machine be repaired or replaced. In some ways, a successful homemaker has a lot in common with a small business owner.

"Business is the office, friendship is the dining room, and intimacy is the bedroom".

—A coparenting counselor

Intimacy. Intimacy is the deep, loving relationship people want with their partners and spouses. When intimacy is positive, there is love and tenderness, protection, nurturance, deep respect, and loyalty. Emotions can be intense. People might know one another so well they can finish each other's sentences, anticipate how they will react, and what they need. With intimates, people want to feel secure, share their lives and their hearts. Here is where people are the most invested and vulnerable because they know each other's deepest feelings, fears, hopes, and dreams. When people are intimate, they can count on each other.

NEGATIVE INTIMACY—THE DARK SIDE

So far, it's all been about the positive sides of business, friendship, and intimacy. There are also the negative sides. There are difficult coworkers, friends who gossip about you, and an intimate who betrays you.

Positive Intimacy a deep positive connection	**Negative Intimacy** a deep negative connection
Highest Levels **Love, Joy, Contentment, a Shared Life**	**Highest Levels** **Hate, Disrespect, Obsession, Addiction**
1. Emotional haven. I feel safe.	1. This conflict is incredibly stressful, full of hate. Sometimes I'm afraid of the other person, sometimes of my own emotions.
2. It's the best kind of intense.	2. It's intense. And not in a good way.
3. We know what to expect from one another.	3. I know exactly what he/she is thinking, and it's not good.
4. I'm accepted, respected, and appreciated.	4. I am disrespected, humiliated.
5. I totally trust my partner to be loyal, honest, and reliable.	5. I can't trust him/her to be honest or follow agreements.
6. We admire and support each other and give each other the benefit of the doubt.	6. He/she tells lies about me to others. Thinks the worst about me.
7. I trust my partner to do the right thing for the right reasons.	7. Tries to cheat me or keep the children from me.
8. We work out our differences and we can agree to disagree.	8. He/she is a troublemaker and unreasonable.
9. We look after each other. We are there for one another.	9. He/she threatens and tries to bully me.
10. We can give and take and don't keep score.	10. He/she tries to know my business, control me. Keeps score.
11. I feel relaxed and content.	11. I feel exhausted, emotionally drained.

Negative intimacy is when an intimate relationship has turned hostile. It is the flip side of positive intimacy behavior. *But it is still intimacy.* Everyone seems to have a least a little of this "bad blood" negative intimacy before and after they separate. People are still deeply attached and invested emotionally but in a hurtful way. Instead of loyalty, there is disloyalty. Instead of trust, there is distrust. Instead of acceptance, there is rejection. No one knows how to hurt you as deeply as a former intimate. Negative intimacy is more than a momentary irritation or a flash of anger. It has an edge with momentum, an emotional punch that can spiral into an intense (but negative) emotional connection. It has the power to keep "enemies" attached to one another. Some people may think that when they hate or are disgusted with the other person that it is proof that they are not attached anymore. But their strong emotions give them away. The opposite of "love" is not "hate," it's neutral, with no intense emotions one way or the other.

Negative intimacy can be at a low level, simmering under the surface. It can grow to become more and more intense.

Divorce Handcuffs

Negative intimacy has the power to keep "enemies" attached to one another with emotional handcuffs. The opposite of "love" is not "hate," it's neutral, with no intense feelings one way or the other.

The Negative Intimacy Spiral

Many if not most couples struggle with negative intimacy, sometimes for many months or even years. It's understandable. People are in deep pain and it's difficult to think straight. It's easy to sink into negative intimacy over just about anything. It can be over big issues like child support or how many days or overnights they should have with the children. But it can also begin over garden-variety events that are annoying, even somewhat unfair. A Dad grumbles that Mom doesn't help the kids bring all their schoolwork to his place, and he slips into negative intimacy as he thinks about the times he has had to drive to her house to pick up homework because she forgot to remind the kids to pack it. Within a few minutes he is furious and sends off a nasty email to her. Perhaps Mom is irritated that Dad makes such a big deal out of the forgotten homework. When she reads his email, she becomes more and more angry as she thinks about how he likes to find fault with her, so she shoots off a blistering answer.

. . . picking at every little thing is a way to keep the negative attachment going and not worth the hassle.

Hopefully one or both of them will come to realize eventually that picking at every little thing is a way to keep the negative attachment going and not worth the hassle. But sometimes, this insight is slow coming. There are other ways to solve irritations. Besides, they could save their energy for other more serious issues.

Negative Intimacy
Can Be Addictive

Even though intense emotion and confusion is a common but painful reaction to separation or divorce, after a while that negative intimacy behavior can become an addiction. Because their negative intimacy spiral started several years before they separated, both Cody and Laura are addicted to seeing each other in a negative way. When people freeze their negative beliefs about someone, they can't really hear what the other person is saying or give credit to his or her positive attitudes or actions. One or both of them can't consider information that would question their negative beliefs about the other. To make matters worse, negative intimacy can become a powerful and destructive drug. Most of us know someone who has made their experience of negative intimacy the main story about their life.

Danger

If left untreated, negative intimacy addiction can injure the adults and traumatize the children. The longer it sticks around and the more intense it is, the deeper and nastier it can get. Trying to turn it around is a major, sometimes impossible task. A marriage can end, but divorce, when there are children, is forever. And if you're stuck in negative intimacy, it's hell. It's worth the effort to neutralize its effect on you and get on with your life.

Learn How Negative Intimacy Operates in Your Life

Do any of the following things happen to either you or your coparent?

**WARNING
IS DANGEROUS TO YOUR
NEW RELATIONSHIP**

Negative intimacy can easily contaminate your chances of having a successful new relationship. When someone spends negative energy on a former partner, this takes away energy and time from a new partner—unless that partner also buys into the negative intimacy system. It's no wonder that many potential partners of recently divorced persons break it off. Anger and resentment strain the new relationship. Besides, if someone can be so hateful toward or pushed around by a former spouse, that person can also turn on them down the road. Who wants all that trouble, anyway?

✓ Your Negative Intimacy Inventory

Does the other parent do this? Does the other parent say that you do this?	Does the other parent do this?			Does the other parent say you do this?		
	NO	SOME	YES	NO	SOME	YES
1. Pays too much attention to my personal life, especially who I'm dating. Asks the kids too many questions about me.	○	○	○	○	○	○
2. Thinks the worst about me. Jumps to the wrong conclusions before checking things out.	○	○	○	○	○	○
3. Is disrespectful, angry, bitter, mean-spirited, or sarcastic—sometimes in front of the kids or with others.	○	○	○	○	○	○
4. Seems to be in competition with me. Is more interested in making me wrong than in doing what's good for our child.	○	○	○	○	○	○
5. Trying to talk often brings up hard feelings, arguments, or more problems.	○	○	○	○	○	○
6. Won't answer my calls, email, or texts, OR is in constant contact for every little thing.	○	○	○	○	○	○
7. I have frequent intense or negative feelings about the other parent.	○	○	○	○	○	○
8. Brings up our history together—who's to blame, what did or didn't happen.	○	○	○	○	○	○
9. Won't follow all of our court orders or Parenting Plan or Agreements.	○	○	○	○	○	○
10. Add your own.	○	○	○	○	○	○
11. Add your own.	○	○	○	○	○	○

How to Use Your Answers

"No" answers are important strengths in your coparenting partnership. Congratulations! As you read the rest of this chapter and the ones that follow, make a mental note about what you do that keeps you out of the muck of negative intimacy.

"Not Sure" answers are Yellow Flags. Slow down. Sometimes a "Not Sure" answer is because a person hasn't really considered a question before. Other times it's because the situation only happens once in a while. Things might change after you read the rest of this book and put some of the tools into practice.

A "Yes" answer to Question 9 can mean serious trouble. People must follow agreements and court orders, or both of you must agree to a change in those agreements even if one of you feels the agreement is unfair or it is hard to follow. Talk to a counselor or an attorney and try to get this resolved.

Other "Yes" answers are red flags. If you have any "Yes" answers and things do not improve after you try some of the tools in this book, seriously consider working with a counselor. In the meantime, pay special attention to the very important strategies and guidelines explained in the rest of this chapter and the next one. "Yes" answers can handcuff you the other parent.

You can't control the other parent. But you can control yourself.

Is Negative Intimacy Getting You What You Want?

Negative intimacy is probably not getting you what you want and it certainly isn't good for your child. But for some people negative intimacy is better than no intimacy at all. Look over the steps below for some ideas.

HOW TO MANAGE NEGATIVE INTIMACY AND GET BACK IN CONTROL

To begin the strategies and guidelines process, look at this next image with Intimacy, Friendship, and Business, this time with a big arrow. The arrow takes off from the "Intimacy" side, skipping over "Friendship" and landing on "Business." Why? Because separation and divorce call for shifting your emotional gears from one way of relating to a different way.

What are your choices? You are still parents and you need to relate about the children, but you can't be intimate anymore. Being friends, as good as that may sound, rarely works out to begin with, so what's left is a special kind of business relationship. This is not your ordinary job-related relationship. This is special because it is about your children. Read on to see how this can work for you.

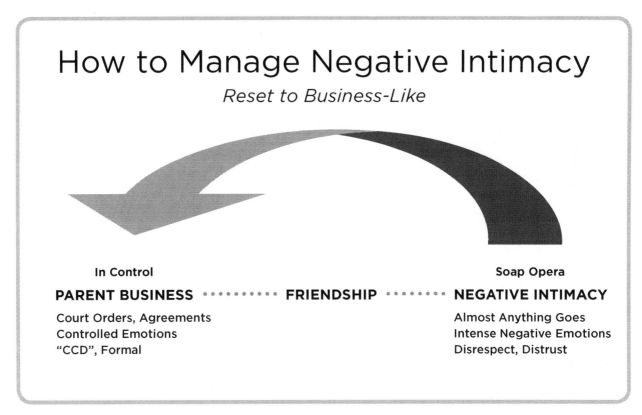

How to Manage Negative Intimacy
Reset to Business-Like

In Control		Soap Opera
PARENT BUSINESS · · · · · · · **FRIENDSHIP** · · · · · · · **NEGATIVE INTIMACY**		
Court Orders, Agreements		Almost Anything Goes
Controlled Emotions		Intense Negative Emotions
"CCD", Formal		Disrespect, Distrust

Step One: Shift Your Focus to Business When You Talk to or Think about the Other Parent

Move from the negative emotional connection to the "public" and less emotional structure of "business." It may seem quite strange at first to think "business," but it has a good chance to work if you take the time to understand it and then stick with it. The road to understanding means taking the time to read the rest of this chapter and the next one carefully where you will find many "How-To" guides, tips, and examples.

· ·

Being Friends?

Maybe. In time. When parents first develop a reasonable business-like working relationship, there's a better chance at eventual friendship down the road.

· ·

Step Two: Use the Power of Your Rational Brain

- **Think about the other parent only as your child's other parent not as a former lover.** Perhaps you can't do this very well right now, but if you want to move on you will have to, bit by bit, learn how to eventually control how you react (at least on the surface), even if the other parent never does make this change.

- **Try helping yourself with positive thoughts.**

  - **"I control my own negative intimacy."** This reminder may help with your determination for a better life.

  - **"I can't control the other parent."** Could you control the other parent when you were together? Probably not. He or she might change if you do, but don't count on it. It's easy to think that if you just try what you did before only now put in more effort, that this time you will actually get him or her to change. But, keep this in mind. If it didn't work before, it probably won't work now either.

- **Watch to see if and how your negative emotions control the way you relate to the other parent.** Negative emotions are very powerful and can easily shut down our rational brain and constructive thinking. If you learn how to use certain business-like skills, for example with communications, emails, and meetings, you can gradually regain control. Find your own pace with this. One small step at a time. A reminder: If your feelings of negative intimacy start to take over, talk to your best friend, write in a journal, work out, talk to yourself, but try not to blow up at the other parent.

> Tip: Brain research shows that when you give your feelings a name or write them down, they can lose some of their negative punch and you can be more in control.

Step Three: Prepare for Feeling Strange at First

You have history with the other parent where you probably shared deep emotions and a complex life. How can you act as if this never mattered? Intimacy—both positive and negative—has been your way of living with this person. Now, you're supposed to just act business-like? Not easy. In fact, you may not be able to even think about this at first.

It may feel dishonest to act reserved and businesslike when actually inside you are fearful, hurt, or resentful and want him or her to know it. But look to the future. If you continue to wage a cold war or let loose with your feelings (or allow him or her to do this to you), where will that get you? Will it get you back together? Will it lead to a better coparenting relationship? Will it be good for your children? Will it really be good for you in the long run—after the short-lived satisfaction of "letting it all out"?

Step Four: When Will You Be Ready to Act Business-Like?

Do you need to be in a certain emotional place before you can act business-like with the other parent? Or do you just go ahead and act the part and hope it works? In other words, what comes first? Changing how you feel or changing how you act? Some people believe that their behavior will only change if their feelings change first. But, research has shown that changing your behavior can actually help change how you feel.

Try this. Act as if the other parent is a very important person at your job. You know you must be on your best behavior no matter how you feel. You have to be calm, courteous, and diplomatic. You already know how to do that at work. Now, take that experience and teach yourself how to use it when you meet, talk, text, tweet, or email the other parent. We don't have to be furious with someone to retreat from intimacy. Close that window to your heart of hearts gently and respectfully. In the next chapter there's a whole section on grief and grieving and our deeper emotions like sadness and loss.

Step Five: Read about Business Guidelines in the Next Chapter

The next chapter has expanded time-tested guidelines, tips, strategies, and tools for managing negative intimacy and explains various options for managing parent-business. If you had a lot of "Yes" answers on the Negative Intimacy Inventory Quiz, try to read this chapter and the next chapter once a day for the next four weeks. Stay with it. Trying to change our way of thinking and behaving takes effort and persistence. You may not be able to change the other parent, but you can gain more emotional freedom by acting differently yourself.

Question: Why can't we be friends as coparents now? Why does it have to be "business"?

Answer: Every situation is different and trying to be friends might work for a while, but over the first few years when there's a setback in the legal process, a remarriage, new baby, or a job setback, it's common for old negative intimacy attitudes to flare up. Unfortunately, the second time around can be just as bad or worse as the first time. Instead, if you are successful at developing a business-like working partnership over

> **Divorced "To" or Divorced "From"?**
>
> Do you want to be divorced TO your former partner or divorced FROM them? If you want to be divorced FROM them, learn how to neutralize your own "negative intimacy." Don't get handcuffed to the other parent.

*When I first read about
the "business" approach
and negative intimacy
and then started
using it when I talked
to the other parent,
I had no idea that it
would change my life
so quickly. But it did.
I was struggling with
my relationship with
my child's father, but
after this, I knew what
to do. I didn't always
do it, but I knew it was
the right thing to do.*

*—A coparent divorced
for one year*

two years or so, this can gradually rebuild some of the lost trust and respect. Then, it gets easier to have more give and take for the sake of the kids, to be more flexible, to hear each other out. Friendship may come about naturally, but it is a new type of friendship. Your first step, though, is to let go of intimacy and develop a business-like partnership as parents.

Question: What if I am able to develop this business-like approach, but the other parent seems determined to behave in a negative intimacy way?

Answer: Stay with your neutral business-like approach. We can't change other people, but if you stay the course, your child will have your example of how to manage difficult situations and still keep your dignity and self-respect. Perhaps the other parent will agree to have a session or two with a coparent counselor to try and find a solution or at least commit to a Limited CoParenting arrangement. If the other parent's behavior continues to be way out of line, perhaps coparenting is not a good idea. Before you make that kind of decision, be sure to get some professional help. In any case, no matter what the other parent does, you can manage your own behavior in a healthy way. And read *Appendix 9: When You Have Done All You Can Do.*

The Most Important Tool for Successful CoParenting

Developing a respectful business-like parenting relationship is probably the most important tool in this Toolkit because it can be a roadmap for how to interact. As you become more and more comfortable with it, it's easier to communicate, solve problems, keep your child out of the middle, and find ways to work with each other's parenting style—all of which can benefit you, your child, and your new life.

NOTE FOR CHAPTER 4

1. This chapter builds on the original concepts in *Mom's House, Dad's House: Making Two Homes for Your Child*, pp. 76–93.

CHAPTER
5

Use Special Business Guidelines for Relating to the Other Parent

How to Be "Business-Like"
The Parent-Business Guidelines
Tips for Following the The Parent-Business Guidelines
What Are Your Personal Boundaries?
Grief and Grieving—It's Not Easy but Necessary
Getting to a Relaxed Business Relationship

The last chapter laid the foundation for parent "business-like" behavior. This chapter shows you ways you can put that into practice. Just like learning anything new, it will take time and practice. A reasonable "business-like" approach actually can become the most efficient path to achieving your new "normal" life. It is also the most effective way to implement the Basic CoParenting Guidelines and the Limited CoParenting Guidelines. This approach can also give you the tools on how to be "CCD"—Calm, Courteous, and Diplomatic—one of the most important skills to have as a parent and coparent.[1]

CCD—I will keep trying to be calm, courteous, and diplomatic.

HOW TO BE "BUSINESS-LIKE"

Focus on Doing What's Best for the Children

Remember the arrow going from negative intimacy to a business-like relationship from the last chapter? That's your destination. As you to move toward your goal, you'll find that some things will be the same as when you were parenting together under the same roof, but other things will probably be different. Here is a beginning list of tools for how you can take control of negative intimacy, heal, and build a healthy coparenting relationship.

PARENT-BUSINESS GUIDELINES

- Follow the Guidelines for Effective CoParent Communications in the next chapter for picking the right words, place, times, and attitude.
- Use extra effort to keep emotions in check. No drama, sarcasm, criticism, blaming, or acting the victim. Don't let negative intimacy win.
- Ask yourself what you would do if the other parent was a co-worker at your job and it was mandatory that you find a way to work together. How would you act?
- Keep your relationship as parents separate from how you relate as former partners.
- Keep your personal life private (especially dating) and on a need-to-know basis if it affects the children.
- Pick your battles. Let little things go. Give the other parent the benefit of the doubt in small things.
- Make no assumptions about plans and doublecheck them.
- Decide on parent-business hours.
- Be on time. Have children ready on time.
- Have an organized schedule for sharing times. Use a calendar.

- Find ways to peacefully resolve disagreements. Rebuild trust by being trustworthy. Try the strategies in Chapter 8 for solving problems.
- Avoid using "hard-ball" tactics.
- Review the Limited CoParenting Guidelines from Chapter 2 and pick any guideline from that list that feels right for you now.
- Be the best parent you can be.

The Affair

If your relationship ended because of an affair, the pull of intense painful and negative feelings can be overwhelming for both parents. It's one of the most emotional experiences imaginable. Try to find a way to allow yourself to grieve so you can eventually move on. As difficult as it might be—and you may not want to hear or think about this right now—that intimate relationship with the other parent is not in your life anymore. He or she is no longer yours. The good news is that your family is still a family, even though it's not put together in the same way as before. Do your utmost to eventually break free of bitterness and contempt about the pain and guilt you have suffered. Your children need you emotionally healthy and back on your feet. Fortunately, a business-like approach, when you are able to take it on, can help you put your life together again.

TIPS

FOR FOLLOWING
THE PARENT-BUSINESS GUIDELINES

Love your kids more than you dislike the other parent.

■ Doing business with someone you don't like or trust

In business, you might be able to avoid working with someone you don't like or trust, but often you have to find a way to make it work. If you can't, you probably have to find another job. In coparenting, this is your precious child. You are the parent. You can't just quit and fade away. Instead, you will just have to find a way to work out something with the other parent.

■ Walking the tightrope

Those first months when people are trying to tear themselves loose from both positive and negative intimacy can be like walking a tightrope. You know you will always be more to one another than just a business partner because you have children together. But you can't be intimates either and friendship at this stage is unlikely, so it's "business" by default. Some people pick up on how to be business-like quickly and put it into practice. But for most people, it takes a lot longer. It can feel unnatural and dishonest to use the business-like idea and try and be calm, courteous, and diplomatic. So they can't or don't do it—at least not for a while. This is especially true if, like Laura, you feel deeply betrayed and discarded by your former mate or like Cody who feels overwhelmed with Laura's threats and complaints.

In your mind and heart, it might help to picture your former mate in a new "place." One that is different from what it was before, one that has a big sign over it, "My child's other parent." When you talk about him or her, don't use their given name, say instead, "My child's mother" or "My child's father." This can help put things in a new perspective. These are your reminders that this is your child's parent and no longer your spouse. Be patient with yourself. Just keep trying and re-read this Toolkit often. When you slip backwards, just try again later. If you find that coparenting has become unhealthy, then be sure to read *Appendix 9, When You Have Done All You Can Do.*

Caution: Although this chapter has been about finding a way to relate to the other parent, your efforts should not ignore a situation where there is risk to you or your child because of the other parent's behavior or threats. As mentioned at the beginning of the book, there are situations where coparenting is not a good idea and toxic for you and your child. Coparenting should not be used as a way for this sad situation to continue.

■ Tips from other parents

You've probably worked at different jobs, so you know how you might act with a difficult boss or co-worker. Here are some tips from some other parents who used what they learned at work to get along with the other parent.

TIPS

ON HOW TO GET ALONG WITH THE OTHER PARENT

YOUR IDEAS

TIPS FROM OTHER PARENTS

■ Be very, very careful what you say and do. Don't just jump in.

■ Don't be a robot when you talk. You have to be real.

■ When things are tense, don't talk to each other in person or even over the phone. Use email, or texts.

■ Try to not upset the other parent. It doesn't help anyone, especially not your child.

■ Play it cool and set limits, like no contacts after 7 p.m.

■ Before you write or call, think things through. Make everything brief. Stick to that subject.

■ Realize that he (or she) will probably not change and that if that happens, it won't be for you—although some changes might be for the children.

■ Don't take the bait to start a fight.

■ When I think she (or he) is lying to me, I only ask a few questions. Then, I let it go. Life's too short. But if it hurts the kids, that's different.

■ Put important things in writing so they can't be twisted around to say something "never happened."

■ Don't embarrass your kids by acting immature.

■ Don't use the day-to-day tasks of caring for your child to play a game of "gotcha." That's a negative-intimacy dance disguised as childrearing. No competing.

Negative Intimacy Is Like A Leaky Boat

Out-of-control negative intimacy is like being in a leaky rowboat about a mile off shore from where your kids are stranded all alone. The parents know they must get to shore somehow, but they argue about who bails out the water and who rows. The longer they argue, the more water the boat takes on and the farther it drifts out to sea. The solution: Make your priority the children, not which one of you is right.

That Small Flicker of Hope
That You Might Get Back Together

When you get emotional with the other parent, you strengthen that old intimate connection. An emotional exchange is a connection even if it's negative. Sometimes, at a deep level, there might be a small flicker of hope that since there is still so much emotion there, just maybe things might resolve and you can get back your dream of a happy family. Just remember, even if you think this dream may come true, do not even suggest that you might get back together to your child until it is a true reality. It is not fair to them.

Healing from Negative Intimacy

Be kind to yourself. It takes time to deactivate and readjust our emotions with the other parent. We may not be able to actually erase memories but we can learn how to turn down their ability to take over our reactions. It will take an open mind and effort, but even though you can't change the other parent, you can heal yourself for your own mental health and for your child. Only you can decide not to be intimate anymore.

WHAT ARE YOUR PERSONAL BOUNDARIES?

Some parents have fluid boundaries with the other parent about their property and their personal lives. For some people, the things listed below are convenient, comforting, or supportive. For others, however, they are intrusive and confusing. If you do any of the following, ask yourself, why? Is it for convenience sake, for mutual support, or is it actually a way to stay emotionally connected and not move on? You decide which it is in your case and whether it is helping your children.[2]

If you couldn't influence the other parent when you were married, do you honestly expect to influence them after divorce? When you let that go and focus just on the business of caring for your children, things get easier.

—A Dad

☐ You have a key to the other parent's home and vice versa.

☐ You have a key to the other parent's car and vice versa.

☐ You and the other parent feel free to drop by the other's home without calling first (when it's not part of a transition arrangement).

☐ You or the other parent feel free to come into one another's home without invitation to get something for a child.

☐ You share detailed personal information about your social, financial, or work/professional life with the other parent.

Return of the Keys

Monika and Roberto have keys to each other's homes so they can get something for the kids when the other parent is not at home. Last week, Monika explained to Roberto that she would feel more comfortable if they would return each other's keys. Roberto feels he has always called or texted Monika before coming over and he is insulted. It bothers him that she doesn't trust him enough to keep things the way they are. Monika replies that things have changed now that she has a serious relationship and that she needs more privacy. They return their keys, but Roberto is feeling pushed away and he doesn't like it.

You've Changed. So Has the Other Parent

Even several years after your separation, it is natural to have some negative assumptions which may include thinking, "This is the way he/she acts. I lived with him/her all those years. I know him/her." However, you are not altogether the same people you were then—for better or for worse. Keep that in mind. Both of you probably changed from your wedding day to the time you separated. And with the demands of single parenting, legalities, negotiations, new jobs, and new loves, you have probably changed even more. If either of you have that habit of "freezing" your view of your former mate in an old block of time, this can stand in the way of useful communications and negotiations.

GRIEF AND GRIEVING:
IT'S NOT EASY, BUT NECESSARY

A dying relationship is torture, and the separation and divorce is a death. The disintegration of an intimate relationship raises questions and emotions that are profound. It takes time to understand what happened, to mourn your losses, and to deal with necessary changes. People not only say goodbye to their intimate relationship, but also to full-time with their child, a lifestyle, the dream of a happy marriage, perhaps their home, neighborhood, friendships, social circles, and other people and circumstances that were deeply important and meaningful. Just because millions of people have divorced doesn't mean that it's easy. A heart attack is also common, but it's not easy. People can feel depressed, empty, adrift, powerless, frustrated, trying to make sense of what happened, perhaps fixated on what "should have been."

Grieving is normal . . . Be good to yourself. If you do some self-assessment, things should ease up in time.

Grieving is not easy, but it is natural if you allow it to run its course. Healthy grieving involves private "review work"[3] of the past and gradually coming to terms with what you experienced and moving on. The catch with separation and divorce is that as you grieve, those intense negative intimate feelings can develop and take over temporarily. Negative feelings are normal, but when we grieve they can be so intense that they cover up and push away the softer, deeper feelings like remorse, sorrow, true loss, and longing. Why are these vulnerable feelings important? Because, when you get in touch with them, you help yourself truly heal.

What to do? Accept that grieving is normal and that you will have your unique way of healing. Be good to yourself. If you do some self-assessment, things should ease up in time. One of my clients said he felt like a combination of three people: One a private person full of emotion and grief, mourning the loss of the dream of a happy marriage and children and sometimes still feeling attached to his wife. The second was the one that is angry, fed up, ready to do battle, get revenge, or the opposite—cave in, give up, pretend the changes are not all that important, do nothing. The third person was the "public" person who learned how to be controlled, calm, courteous, and diplomatic with the other parent. A "public" part of you can also help you using the business-like approach to build a parent team for your children and keep a structure and routine going at home for your children. There's an unexpected bonus: The structure of the business approach, if you stay with it, can actually give you more internal room to process your grief better.

Let it all out or hold it all in? We can and should express our feelings—but to ourselves and to selected others. We need to do this safely. For some people this is obvious. But for others "letting it all out" feels like a free pass to have a meltdown, a mean-spirited conversation or email that goes to the "ex" and maybe also to friends, mutual acquaintances, or neighbors. But wait, holding it all in isn't healthy, either. There exists a safer middle ground between letting it all out and holding it all in. Talk to your very closest friends, people who will keep your confidences. If you have deeply powerful emotions, take care of yourself and see a therapist or a trained professional at your place of worship. There are gentle and supportive ways to help you grieve and sort things out.

How do people keep their feelings under control—besides counseling, deep breathing, meditation, or punching a wall? Remember these options, too. Write in a journal, talk to yourself, get plenty of exercise (which will help your depression and circulation), or join a class or group on parenting or divorce recovery. Take care of yourself first!

Find Your Balance and Live Your Life

Find your balance between questioning and examining your feelings of grief and just living your life. This period of time is a major challenge and you need to be able to look at it from the outside and even laugh at it once in a while. Just keep working on your skills for a business-like approach for those contact times with the other parent. This can help your grief run its natural course.[4]

GETTING TO A RELAXED BUSINESS RELATIONSHIP

As time passes and parents continue to be courteous and businesslike, the level of formality seems to relax, and threats and hurts of the past are softened or neutralized. Consistent practice of business relationship skills breeds courteous communication between coparents which can ease the stress and make for more flexibility with the schedule and responsibilities. There are many rewards for staying the course. Some examples: It will be easier for one parent to fill in when the other parent has to work out of town, or when a child asks to stay longer at one home.

Find your balance between grieving, just living your life, and planning for your future.

Getting Along—The Benefits of Using a Business Approach

1. Uses the skills and insights that you already have about relationships at work and applies them to your new coparenting role.
2. Gives you suggested ground rules and guidelines for relating to the other parent.
3. Gives you tools to identify and then manage destructive emotions about the other parent and in yourself.
4. Gives you tips and strategies that you can also use at work, especially with coworkers and supervisors.
5. Gives you the tools for upholding the Basic CoParenting Guidelines for building and maintaining a healthy coparenting relationship.

How children can bounce back from their parents' negative intimacy. When the children see two people they love eventually working together and showing mutual respect, it is a relief! And they also learn lessons about how to turn a bad situation into one that's tolerable. It gives them hope that no matter how hurtful and desolate things might be, their parents have taught them by example how to work things out and make a new and happy family life. Even if only one parent succeeds at neutralizing their own negative behavior and attitude, children can feel more secure and can watch and learn important skills.

It might take months, a year, sometimes much longer, but many couples can make the transition to a reasonable working relationship. Children can learn from your example that situations and even difficult personal relationships can be defused enough for a higher cause, such as a healthier and happier family for everyone.

The Ride of Your Life and Moving On

When people live together, they learn from each other—for better or for worse. They can share good times and bad ones and become a part of each other's lives. If they separate, those experiences don't automatically disappear. These memories will still come up now and then. The feelings that go with them aren't necessarily a sign that the separation was a mistake or that they are a sure sign of negative intimacy. Instead, these memories seem to be a combination of grief, the pain of losing the dream of one happy family indivisible, and all the requirements to readjust to another way of living. Your relationship will always be more than casual. Your former relationship did matter, but now it's restructured differently. You continue to parent together, but no longer as romantic partners.

> "You have no idea of all the benefits you get personally," said one mother who had been coparenting successfully for ten years. "There's greater health, happiness, a better relationship with your child, and with your own life and activities."

Question: My wife left me for another man. If I treat her with respect and am business-like, I'm feeling like I'm saying what she did was OK.

Answer: It's normal to be very upset especially under the circumstances. What she did, however, is something between you adults. Put aside your own feelings for a moment and ask yourself if you want your children to respect and love their mother? If you put her down to the kids or are disrespectful to her in front of the kids, you are involving them in your adult issues. This is not fair to them. They can't fix what happened or find justice for you. She is their mother and they will have a relationship with her for the rest of their lives.

How best can you and your children move on? What would you do if you were seriously injured in a freak accident by a violent storm and had to be hospitalized? You were expected to make full recovery but only after treatments and rehabilitation. Once you recovered from the shock of it all, would you spend your energies on the treatments and rehabilitation or on feeling victimized and powerless? In order to get on with your life, set your sights on acting business-like. You may not be successful right away, but the big key is to keep at it. You can't change how she treated you, but you can change how you react to her now, and by doing so you are in charge of yourself. Otherwise, her past behavior can still have power over your life now.

The most important thing is to find healthy ways to neutralize or control conflict with the other parent and work toward becoming a parent team. This is true regardless how you divide or share time with your child.

• •

Discouraged?

Take heart. There is a way through this. Do the best you can, and if you stumble, just right yourself and begin again. As long as your children are not at risk and you see some progress, it's worth the effort.

• •

NOTES FOR CHAPTER 5

1. This chapter builds on and updates the original concepts in *Mom's House, Dad's House*, pp. 94–112.

2. In *Mom's House, Dad's House*, there is another self-test on pp. 87–88 that is also helpful. It is entitled "Are You Moving Away from Intimacy?"

3. See a full description of "review work" in *Mom's House, Dad's House* on pp. 62–66.

4. Children also grieve. See *Mom's House, Dad's House*, pages 146–147, 152, and *Mom's House, Dad's House for KIDS*, pages 11–23 on feelings and "special energy."

CHAPTER

6

Try These Tools to Side-Step Communication Potholes

Keep Each Other Up to Date
Guidelines for Effective CoParent Communication
Prepare for Meetings and E-Contacts
Manage Your Stress
Guidelines for Limited CoParenting Communication
Acknowledge the Other Parent's Strengths
Guidelines for E-Etiquette

KEEP EACH OTHER UP TO DATE

The lifeblood of coparenting is the right kind of communication. But even after months of effort with coparenting, there can still be times when it's a challenge to stay calm, courteous, and diplomatic. Those negative intimacy feelings can skulk around off and on for a long time and get in the way of sharing important information about your children.

Even when communicating with the other parent is difficult or uncomfortable, coparents still need to keep each other up to date about their children's lives. This is true even if you are in a "Limited CoParenting" arrangement. Use the tools in this chapter to help you and the other parent develop a routine for talking about your children and doing it in a way that doesn't stir up problems.[1]

One father who successfully coparented for years advised, "Don't discount communications with the other parent. This needs to be a priority. Not because it's your former spouse trying to reach you, but because it's your children's other parent. Just because you long ago moved away from negative intimacy, you still need to have a serious and respectful relationship as parents. Learn the difference."

Good communications are the lifeblood of successful and healthy coparenting.

GUIDELINES

FOR EFFECTIVE COPARENT COMMUNICATIONS

The focus is on your child

1   **Keep each other up to date. That probably means you need to exchange information at least once a week.** This is especially important in a "Limited CoParenting" situation. Check out the details in "Limited CoParenting Communications" later in this chapter.

2   **Share certain information your child tells you.**[2] Advise your child that with certain topics (such as discipline, allowances, or behavior) you will feel free to share this information with the other parent. It's essential the children know when their parents will keep their confidences and when they will share information with the other parent.

3   **Set your own guidelines for phone calls, meetings, expectations for replies to emails, texts.** Talk about reasonable limits. Examples:

- Emergency contacts should be able to be received at any time.
- Non-emergency contacts should not come before or after certain times. You decide those times.
- Calls at work are (or are not) okay.
- Answering a text or an email should happen within a certain period of time. You decide that time window.
- Texts, emails, or phone calls. When do you feel "overloaded" by them? When do you feel important information is not passed on to you? You decide what is necessary.
- Financial or other adult topics should not be mixed in with discussions about the kids. Keep these separate.

4   **Use reminders.** Kids (and parents) need reminders. A calendar? A cell phone calendar that automatically updates?

....

Did you hear what I said?
People want to know if they were understood and if what they said meant anything to you.

....

The family calendar is useful but it's rarely perfect. Put important things in writing! Just talking about it can be misinterpreted, ignored, or just not even heard at all.

5 **Speak for yourself and get information yourself.** Please do not ask or expect your child to talk for you, spy, or get information. If you do, your child can be caught in the miserable middle. More about this in Chapter 7 and in *Mom's House, Dad's House* on pages 98–103 and *Mom's House, Dad's House for KIDS*, pages 36-44.

6 **Take everything you hear from your child about the other parent with a grain of salt.** Kids are good observers usually, but not always reliable interpreters. More about this in the next chapter.

7 **Prepare for meetings, texts, tweets, and emails.** Use the Guides in this chapter.

8 **Keep information about the other parent confidential.** Do not post, tweet, text, or copy anything that's confidential between you to anyone—not even a friend or relative unless you or your child are in danger and you need help.

Confidentiality

You can exchange confidential information with professionals if you and the other parent authorize this in writing.

REMINDERS. Remember to send the other parent a brief email "diary" or report of what happened during the time your child was with you. A paragraph usually is enough. **Send the short report *the day before* the transition**. Include written instructions for things like medications, care of injuries. **See *Appendix 2: Parenting Plans, Online Resources, and Referrals*** where you can communicate and network on special websites. **Tell the other parent about other things of importance to your child's world**, such as an illness, an achievement, breaking up with a friend, or a fender bender in a parking lot.

Remember the binder, Journal, or an activity and homework folder that goes back and forth with your child. Many parents use this even if they have a flexible arrangement.

Make sure you each make a copy of everything in that folder for yourself. Kids lose things. Parents lose things. Some things from school or the classroom are online, others are not.

Moving in Together:
Monika has told Roberto that Vern will be moving into her home in a few weeks. Until now, Roberto and Monika have been spontaneous with their communications about the children, but Roberto now wants to add a weekly report on the kids and a more formal homework folder that transfers with them. Monika countered with her request of a report from Roberto. Neither parent is willing to be more direct about their concerns about how things might change once Vern moves in. They need to talk. The sooner the better.

Tip: These steps are also helpful when people are preparing for family mediation or meetings with lawyers.

Examples of Effective CoParent Communication

Example 1: Mom emails Dad that Harry's teacher told her that Harry probably needs a tutor in Algebra. She asks Dad what he thinks and they make plans to go together to talk with the teacher.

Example 2: Dad calls Mom around noon to say that 10-year-old Debra had just called him in tears because some girls taunted her about the scars on her arms and pushed her against the bathroom wall. Dad was able to calm Debra but wanted Mom to know about this before Debra came home from school. He asks if she thinks they should report this to the school.

Example 3: Mom and Dad have a binder that they send back and forth with the children. In this binder, they insert notices from school, baseball and Judo schedules, permission slips, and other items to prevent their children missing out on any activities.

PREPARE FOR MEETINGS AND E-CONTACTS

Prepare. Please do not contact the other parent on impulse. Prepare first.

Do a quick review about how to be business-like. If you need to refresh your memory or if you are in a Limited CoParenting situation, do a quick review of the list on "How to Be Business-Like" at the beginning of the last chapter and of the strategies and lists in this chapter.

Talk to yourself and take a few notes. "How would I act at work if I absolutely needed this relationship to work?" "What's my tone, my attitude, my body language?" Be honest with yourself. If you are feeling hostile or if what you say has an edge, even a little "dig" can set you back. A reminder: Be CCD, "I am calm, courteous, and diplomatic." "My focus is on the children only." Finally, make a few notes on why this contact is necessary, and what you want to come out of it. Follow the suggestions below.

Set Up the Meeting or Email Exchange

- Have an agenda and stick to it. Only plan to talk about 1 or 2 topics.
- Avoid meetings longer than 15 minutes if tension runs high.
- If you will use the phone, choose a place or time where your children will not overhear you. If you meet in person, make it a public place.

- Read "Steps to Reaching Agreements" in Chapter 8. This is a very helpful guide for any meeting.
- Remember to be prepared to mention one of the other parent's strengths in your conversation. Give credit where credit is due. This is a big key.
- Be specific, not vague. It saves time and bother in the long run.

Be specific

1. **Vague:** "Molly's piano teacher just set another rehearsal this Saturday for the recital in case you are free to go."
2. **Specific:** "The piano teacher just set another rehearsal for the recital in case you are free to go. It's this Saturday, September 20th, starting at 6:30 p.m. at the church hall and it goes to 7:45 p.m. I'll bring Molly and be there the whole time. The teacher also asked parents to sign up to bring refreshments."

MANAGE YOUR STRESS

When the thought of communicating makes you tense or you are in a conversation and you start to feel anxious, here are some tips.

1. Take 2 or 3 slow deep breaths and give your brain some oxygen so it can think clearly. When we're anxious, oxygen goes to our bodies and away from our brain.
2. Talk to yourself. "I can do this." "My focus is on what's best for the kids." Think CCD: "I'm calm, courteous, and diplomatic."
3. Doublecheck your body, attitude, and voice tone: "What's my attitude? Body language? Facial expression? Am I feeling in control?"
4. Try doing some simple stretches to loosen up those tight muscles and do more deep breathing.

Limited Coparenting Communications

When it is difficult to follow the Basic Coparenting Guidelines while interacting with the other parent, you have to pay more attention to communications. It takes extra effort to to be calm, courteous, and diplomatic, especially when the other person is not. Try to rise above all those emotions and frustrations and don't let the other person pick a fight. The Limited Communication Guidelines that follow also include reminders from both the Basic and the Limited CoParenting Guidelines from Chapters 1 and 2 so you can have these guidelines in one place.

GUIDELINES

FOR LIMITED COPARENTING COMMUNICATION

Remember, your communications are about your child.

- Do not contact the other parent without preparing first. Don't skip this step. Acting on impulse can lead to negative intimacy.
- Be reasonable. Don't use email or a text to say what you wouldn't dare say in person.
- Be sure to send that written update so that it is received the day before the child transitions from your home to their other home. If your child is with you more than a week, send an update at the end of 7 days anyway. Do not rely on your child to keep both of you informed.
- Avoid meeting in person, speaking via phone or voice mail until things have calmed down. Use email and texts until then.
- Carefully follow the Guidelines for Email Etiquette at the end of this chapter.
- Keep communications brief and confidential.
- Keep the parent a real person in your mind. Don't make them into a villain or a "thing."
- Take extra care to show you understand what the other person is saying.
- Pay extra attention to regularly and honestly acknowledge the other parent's loyalty, contribution, and dedication to the children. Be genuine.
- Pick your battles carefully. Ask yourself, how dangerous is this to the kids? Let the less important things pass.
- Avoid dueling emails, texts, or tweets. Agree to disagree.
- Pay attention to what subject or attitude triggers an argument or

feelings of shame or anger in the other parent. Try to not pull these triggers.

- Try to be a peacemaker. Volunteer something the other parent would like even when you don't think you are getting the same treatment.

- Do your job as a parent. Let him or her do the same.

- Use a mediator when your differences are about major issues.

- Do some self-assessment. No one is perfect. The other person can't always be wrong about every little thing. What are you adding to the problem?

- Read, re-read, and digest the guidelines for taking control of negative intimacy in Chapters 4 and 5. Hopefully something there will "click," and you can take another step toward healthier coparenting.

Pick the Best Words

1. **Don't start sentences with "You." This can close the door on positive communications**. A "You" sentence can be received as an attack, a judgment, as disrespect, or as blame even when you don't mean it to. Using the word "You" can just keep the misunderstanding going. Example: "You've forgotten their medicine again" probably won't get you the change you want.

2. **Start some sentences with "I".** Starting a sentence with "I" and then using neutral words can work. "I" means you are speaking for yourself. Just describe the situation without judgment or blame. This makes it easier for the other person to listen to you. *NOTE: In coparenting, it's important to use "I" in combination with neutral or business-like words* as shown below.

3. **Use neutral-sounding or business-like words.** Often words like these can be used in a neutral tone: "observed," "noticed," "concerned," "serious," "wondering," or "heard."

4. **Avoid words that describe emotions** such as "upset," "angry," "sad," "disappointed," "worried," "resentful," and scolding or blaming words.

5. **Avoid using the words "never" or "always."** These words, especially in a situation where you want to be diplomatic, often turn people off.

6. **Don't assume you already know the answer.** Describe a situation briefly and ask questions.

No one is perfect. The other person can't always be wrong about every little thing. What are you adding to the problem?

be business-like

Make Boundaries Clear With Neutral and Business-Like Words

The school calls you complaining that the children's homework folder is not being returned when the children are with the other parent. You ask the school to contact the other parent directly and then advise the other parent via email about the call.

Choose your words carefully. Make the boundaries clear and use neutral or business-like words.

Instead of saying: "You're always forgetting to send the children's homework folder back to school. I'm furious with you for embarrassing the kids this way and the school is fed up, too."

Try Saying: "I wanted to give you a heads up that the school called me to say the children have not had their homework folder four times over the last two weeks. Since these were the days they were with you, I asked them to call you directly about it."

Why? First, by saying "I wanted to give you a heads up . . ." and "I asked them to call you directly . . ." you are taking responsibility for your children's welfare by telling the other parent what you were told and what you did. Make the boundaries clear. This is the other parent's responsibility. The other parent and the school should find the solution, not you. You could offer to help with "If I can help with this, let me know."

ACKNOWLEDGE THE OTHER PARENT'S STRENGTHS

Tell some good news! Give credit where credit is due. In your emails and conversations, mention something positive about your children and the other parent. "Matt was so happy. He kept talking about how you had taught him how to ride the bike." Or "After you worked with Alicia, she seems more interested in practicing the piano." Or "Sam may be following your example and becoming a very good interviewer. I saw him asking coach some good questions at practice last week."

Examples of Trouble and Teamwork

Trouble: "You're late again and you've scared Russell into thinking you wouldn't show up at all. How can you stress your child like this? The least you could do is call!"

Teamwork: "When you came late to pick up Russell, I saw him going back and forth to the window and he kept asking me if you were really going to be here and if you'd texted me. I told him that Dad would never be late on purpose and that you probably got stuck in traffic, but he still acted anxious. What ideas do you have for helping him when you are late?, (*Note: One of the strengths of the parent who was late was that he was usually very reliable. The parent emphasized the other parent's strength to the child by saying that Dad would never "be late on purpose.")*

Trouble: "When you won't even say 'Hello' at baseball practice, Abby is mortified that you are so rude to me. The least you could do is act civil."

Teamwork: "When we are at baseball practice, I get the impression that Abby watches both of us as if we are going to do something to worry her like get into an argument. What do you think about the idea of just saying 'Hello' in a cordial way or wave and smile? Do you think it might ease her mind?"

Cody and Laura

Cody and Laura are now doing their best to keep each other up to date about the children with a weekly email "report," but the intervention for Megan's eating disorder and Matt's medication adjustments have given them more to coordinate and worry about so there are more emails and texts. This means there are more chances for finding fault and for tempers to flare about Cody's girlfriend and who is to blame for issues and problems. These are difficult times for them. However, Megan's counselor is helping both parents remember how important it is for each of them to deal with their personal issues privately so that these personal problems don't spill over into their parenting. They started using the Guidelines for E-Etiquette on the next page and found it very useful.

GUIDELINES

FOR E-ETIQUETTE

The internet is not perfect and no message, tweet, or post is totally confidential. It can be a postcard to the world.

Just the Facts: No Attitude, No Meltdowns, No Arguments

Texts, Emails, Tweets, and FaceBook are quick ways to communicate but also risky. It is very tempting to write things you wouldn't dare say in person. So think "CCD". Remember, it just about the children.

- Make these business-like but not cold. Just the facts. No sarcasm, blaming, or threats.
- Stick to one or two subjects. This is especially important when there's conflict.
- Try to be specific. Avoid general and vague answers.
- Answer within 24 hours if possible. Or say when you will answer.
- Avoid using CAPITALS. They are interpreted as shouting.
- If the exchange is about an agreement, use email so you can have a written record.
- Remember to honor confidentiality. More on this below.

Wait! Before you hit "Send" or post it—

- Re-read your message several times. Ask yourself, is it businesslike? CCD? Confidential?
- Save "Urgent" or "Important" flags or words for those rare occasions that are actually urgent.
- When you reply to an email, hit "reply" instead of "new mail message" to keep the "thread" of a discussion in one place.

More About Emails. Use emails for discussions, negotiating, reaching agreements, and giving detailed updates or reports. They can be archived, filed, or printed. This can save time and frustration later.

- Make your emails short. Long emails may not get read all the way through. They can feel like lectures.
- Spell correctly and punctuate. It's easier to understand. It shows respect for the reader.

- If an email is about an agreement, use bullets or numbers for each action. Be specific. It actually helps people to remember. Here's an example of a Mom confirming an agreement about their daughter's transition to be with Dad. The bullets targeted these points:

  - "She will go with you after band practice on your days."
  - "If you are delayed, she'll come home with me and you'll pick her up here."
  - "You will be sure to text me or her about the time you'll be arriving."

More About FaceBook. Never post any confidential or personal information about the other parent on your wall or your pages—not even to family or close friends. You do not have a right to do that. No exceptions. Even if it's general information about the kids and the other parent like a trip or an event, still mark this information for family and very close friends.

About Texts. Use all the guides above for texts too. Don't overuse texting. It's intrusive and annoying.

More About Twitter. Use all the guides above here too. While you can send private tweets, Twitter is basically public so everyone can join in. Again, like FaceBook and emails, be sure to mark your tweets private and don't tweet about sensitive or confidential information that includes the other parent.

Try to make it a habit to follow the *Basic* and *Limited CoParenting Guidelines* and the *E-Etiquette Guidelines*. It could save you a lot of time and misunderstandings.[3]

. . . .

Words Are Powerful And Expensive

An angry word not spoken is rarely regretted. Be careful what you say and how you say it.

. . . .

NOTES FOR CHAPTER 6

1. This Chapter expands and updates the section on communications in *Mom's House, Dad's House*, pp. 98–102.

2. *Mom's House, Dad's House for KIDS* has a series of "Words to Try" sections for kids listed on p. 250. Parents who read these can gain further insight into how and why children find it difficult to express their feelings and fears.

3. There is a section on direct and indirect communications, responses from the other parent, and assessing your communications on pp. 98–104 in *Mom's House, Dad's House*.

7

Avoid the Miserable
Middle for You and the Kids

The Miserable Middle—No Way Out
Eavesdropping, Telling Tales, Lying, Refereeing
Quiz: Are Children in the Middle?
When Kids Say Things That Raise a Red Flag
Avoiding Negative Intimacy Traps
Trouble or Teamwork

You and the other parent are under constant surveillance—by your children. When they want to, they can pick up on your conversation and body language from across the room, listen and watch keenly your reactions, words, actions, and especially what happens between you and their other parent. Children have feelings and interpretations about what they see and hear. It is their life and you control it in great measure. Remember the saying, "Children are great observers, but poor interpreters." This chapter shares a series of tips and strategies for coping with some of the most common "children in the middle"[1] dilemmas and ways misunderstandings can get out of control.[2]

THE MISERABLE MIDDLE—NO WAY OUT

The middle is a miserable place for a child. Some of the more common dilemmas for children:

— Patti hears her parent's arguments. Patti listens and feels as if there is a fight inside her.
— Elijah's parents are rude to one another, give each other hostile looks when he's around. Elijah feels confused. He may feel a part of him is being insulted, too.
— Paul's mother makes sure that he has his cell phone with him when is with his father so that if he doesn't like something Dad does, he will

call her. Paul feels his mother's fear for him, but feels disloyal to Dad.

— Esther hears Dad make snide comments about her mother to his friends. Esther wonders, "When I grow up will he hate me the way he hates Mom now?"

— Andre's father wants to know if his mother has a boyfriend who stays overnight. Andres knows Dad shouldn't ask about Mom's private life, but he doesn't want Dad to be mad at him so he feels he has to tell him.

— Mom tells Catherine that she has to get that support check from Dad before she comes home. Catherine knows Dad will be mad when she asks and Mom will be mad if she doesn't ask. No matter what she says or does, one parent will make her wrong and yell at her.

— Relatives may put kids in the middle by talking trash about a parent to a child and by showing disapproval when a child talks about their other parent.

The War Inside

Children have both their mother and father within them. The "middle" is where one side of them is hating or at war with the other. Some children feel so torn apart, they must pick a side just to be able to function.

EAVESDROPPING, TELLING TALES, LYING, REFEREEING

When Kids Put Themselves in the Middle

Do any of these sound familiar?

— Diana and Terrel are experts at hiding around corners and eavesdropping when Dad talks to his friend about Mom. Then they tell Mom what they think he said.

— Omar is in middle school. He stands between his mother and father when they argue and shoves them apart, sometimes telling one of them they are wrong.

— John lies to Mom saying that Dad is buying him a car on his 17th birthday, knowing that Mom has said no driving because of his grades.

— 8-year-old Noah tells Mom only part of what happened at Dad's and bends the truth just enough to alarm Mom. Mom calls Dad and accuses him of something that didn't really happen that way.

— Five-year-old Kelly wants to get her parents back together so she lies to Mom that Dad kisses her picture every night and lies to Dad that Mom says she still loves him.

In extreme cases, some kids will get into a parent's emails and written documents. It's understandable even though it is unacceptable. Their life is at stake, and they don't trust their parents to make the best decisions. They want to know what's going on even if they are not yet mature enough to know what the information means or how to use it.

When Family Members Behave Badly.

Laura's father did not approve of Laura's marriage to Cody. Once he learned about Cody's affair, he was outraged. Even though he admits that the girls love and need their father, the grandfather is still sarcastic and critical of Cody in public and in front of the girls—especially at the soccer games. Laura and other family members should speak to the grandfather and explain that his behavior is hard on the girls and a bad example. But, some have convinced themselves that it is not important, or that Cody has it coming, or that it's not their business. So, grandfather's hurtful behavior continues.

In this next Quiz, there are different examples of how parents can shield their children from becoming involved in adult issues. Think about your behavior. Maybe you don't do one or two of these things. What about the other parent? Do you believe that he or she does these things?

✓ Quiz: Are Children in the Middle?

Do you do these things? Does the other parent do these things?	YOU			THE OTHER PARENT		
	TRUE	FALSE	USUALLY	TRUE	FALSE	USUALLY
1. You do not allow your child to get involved in your arguments or encourage him or her to spy, report, or pick sides.	○	○	○	○	○	○
2. Your child does not carry messages between you and the other parent.	○	○	○	○	○	○
3. If a child brings a message from the other parent, you tell your child you will talk to the other parent about it, and you do it.	○	○	○	○	○	○
4. You do not ask the children questions about the other parent's personal life.	○	○	○	○	○	○
5. You do not say disrespectful things about the other parent to the child or where the child might overhear you.	○	○	○	○	○	○
6. You do not encourage your child's angry feelings about the other parent or allow him or her to say disrespectful things about a parent.	○	○	○	○	○	○
7. If your child is old enough, you encourage your child to talk to the other parent about their differences.	○	○	○	○	○	○
8. You never ask your child to keep certain things a secret from the other parent.	○	○	○	○	○	○
9. You do not encourage the child to side with you against the other parent.	○	○	○	○	○	○
10. Add your own here.	○	○	○	○	○	○

How to Use Your Answers

Your Answers for Yourself "True" answers are good for your child. "Usually" may mean that sometimes you slip and put your child in a situation where he or she does not belong. If you have "False" answers, then think of ways to improve.

Your Answers about the Other Parent If you gave "True" answers, here is another way to give credit to the other parent. If you gave "Usually" or "False" answers, then see if the other parent is willing to read this chapter and then talk about it with you. Try to be diplomatic as well as direct. The other parent may not agree with your answers. Use this Quiz as a tool for exploring ways you and the other parent can protect your child from these and similar "middle" situations. If you are working with an attorney or a counselor, you might want to share your answers with him or her.

Monika and Roberto's Answers

Monika and Roberto answered "True" to nearly all the questions. Excellent! The exceptions were two "Usually" answers. Monika thought Roberto sometimes asked Sam questions about her and her boyfriend and Roberto thought that Monika might be asking Sam to not tell him things about the boyfriend. When they separated, the children were so young that situations where the children would be in the middle didn't come up. Now, things could go downhill if they let these suspicions grow. Their commitment and cooperative history should help them work this out. Hopefully, they will use some of the tools they learned in this chapter.

WHEN KIDS SAY THINGS THAT RAISE A RED FLAG

Some children want to know and see more than they should. It's natural to want to be involved in matters that are so central to one's life and happiness, but this doesn't mean that it is healthy or appropriate for them to have information beyond their years.

Heads Up! Red Flags

Even when you are very careful to remain neutral on the outside, children—even the younger ones—pick up on your reactions when they say something about the other parent. "Mommy says we're going on a long vacation and I won't see you for a long time," or "Daddy asked me if your boyfriend stays over," or "Mom said I could go to my friend Rich's overnight," or "Dad said if I was living with him most of the time, he'd let me stay out until midnight on weekends."

HANDLING THE RED FLAGS WITH YOUR CHILD

Step One—Stop before you act. Don't jump to conclusions.

Step Two—Ask questions first:

> **Ask your child** simple questions like, "When did this happen?" or "How do you know this?" but don't be harsh or cross-examine. The child's statement may or may not be correct. There is a good chance that what you hear is not the whole story or even the correct one.

> **Then ask the other parent:**

> "I want to ask you about something our child said" (then repeat what was said). "What are your thoughts on what this is about?" **Then wait for the answer**. Often the answer is fairly simple and can lead to a brief discussion about a child's wishful thinking or twisting the truth, or how easily children, even teens, can misunderstand events.

Step Three—Set boundaries with the other parent if they are needed. For example, an 8-year-old tells Dad that Mom wanted to know if he bought a certain type of luxury car.

> **Words to Try:** Dad can say to Mom, "I want you to know that I will not ask our child questions about your personal life and hope you don't ask her about mine. If you have a question, please just ask me directly."

Step Four—But what if your child did accurately report what happened? Or what if you don't think the other parent is telling the truth?

Words to Try: If you don't think you're getting a straight answer from the other parent, say: "OK. I'll take your answer at face value." Privately add a caution in your internal "trust" column. Sometimes when a parent realizes the other parent has made a good guess, things improve without anyone admitting anything. If twisting or bending the truth is a habit however, then coparenting is in trouble.

AVOIDING NEGATIVE INTIMACY TRAPS

Alicia Felt Humiliated by Mom So How Does Dad Handle It?

Four-year-old Matt and the 12-year-old twins Megan and Alicia have come to their dad Cody's house for the weekend. Matt seems happy. Megan is quiet but Alicia is in tears. Alicia tells her Dad that her mother criticized her in front of her friends and she feels humiliated. What will Cody do now?

Poor Choices: Falling into Negative Intimacy Traps

- Dad assumes Alicia's version of the incident is accurate.
- Dad lets Alicia go on and on blaming her mother.
- Dad becomes more and more upset with Mom as he sees his daughter's pain.
- Dad shoots off an angry email or phone call to Mom using negative intimacy words such as, "I am very upset about the way you criticized Alicia in front of her friends. She was humiliated. You were disrespectful and insensitive, especially since she is so fragile right now!"

Better Choices: Business-Like Communication

- Dad helps Alicia calm down. He does not automatically react to Alicia's intense emotions. Dad knows Alicia well enough to know that she needs to unwind before he can reason with her.
- Once his daughter has calmed down, Dad listens to Alicia and asks a few questions, but does not assume Mom was insensitive and hurtful even if he suspects some of this is true.

- Dad acknowledges Alicia's feelings and perspective but doesn't necessarily agree with her.
- Dad explains that while he is sorry that she is so upset, this is not something he can fix for her because this is between Alicia and her mother.
- Dad suggests that Alicia call or write her mother about how she feels. Dad cautions her to be respectful and calm when she does it. He says he will tell her mother that she is upset but will only tell her that he wants Alicia to talk to her mother about it herself.
- Dad contacts Mom. He starts by saying something positive. *"I thought you should know that Matt came in today on cloud nine saying that the Halloween costume you got for him was the best. But Alicia came in upset because she felt you criticized her in front of her friends. I calmed her down but did not want to discuss it much further with her. I have urged her to talk to you directly about it. She's old enough to discuss this one-on-one with you. If you want to talk further about this, please give me a call."*

CAUTION

If your child fears that the other parent will be overly harsh or abusive if that parent learns what your child has told you, then you may have a serious problem. If you believe your child may be correct, get some expert advice as soon as possible before you talk with the other parent. The last thing you want is to place your child at further risk.

Question: What do I do if my child pleads with me not to tell something to the other parent?

Answer: When your child tells one of you something and wants to keep it a secret from the other parent, it puts you in the middle. The other parent may need to be part of the solution, and it is bad practice for a child to take control of your communications with the other parent. One way to look at this is to ask yourself, "If the situation were reversed, would I want to know this information?" If yes, then don't promise your child you won't tell the other parent. Decide what you will keep confidential with your child and what things you will tell the other parent. As parents, we have an obligation to keep each other informed of issues and incidents that are dangerous or potentially risky. Parents list things like shoplifting, sexual activity, drugs, bullying, poor academics, skipping school, fights, car accidents, lying, depression, threats, cutting, eating issues—the list goes on. A coparent team shares these incidents and worries with one another. Your child needs to know that for certain things you and the other parent work as a team to protect and guide him or her.

TROUBLE OR TEAMWORK

Trouble: Dad tells his teenage daughter that he's fed up with Mom's attitude and that he's thinking of taking her back to court.

Teamwork: Dad tells Mom himself that he wants a good parenting relationship but that what's happening now is not working for him. He suggests a coparent counselor or mediator to help them work things out.

———

Trouble: Dad is late. Mom thinks it's because he forgot that night was dinner night with their son. She assumes he won't show up at all.

Teamwork: Dad is late. Mom calls his cell phone and asks when she should expect him. She doesn't ask why he's late. If the son is old enough, he calls Dad himself—not to scold, but to ask when he will arrive.

———

Trouble: Dad hears his daughter say she has an MD appointment tomorrow. He thinks Mom kept this secret because she doesn't want him to be there with her.

Teamwork: Dad calls Mom and says, "Our daughter said there is an MD appointment tomorrow. What's that about?" Mom answers, "It's not an appointment. We're picking up some acne ointment samples."

———

Trouble: Mom doesn't call her 4-year-old at Dad's house as promised. Dad gets angry, and sends Mom a text saying, "It's criminal the way you forget to call your own child! No good mother does that."

Teamwork: The text says: "Our son waited for your call last evening and asked me perhaps 4–5 times why you didn't call. He seemed upset about it so I tried to reach you. Will you be calling him about this? Is there something you want me to tell him?"

Teamwork is what coparenting is about.
—A coparenting Mom

NOTES FOR CHAPTER 7

1. In *Mom's House, Dad's House for KIDS*, pp. 36–44, there is a major section entitled "The Miserable Middle." It can give parents insight into a child's experience with

various situations and has examples and suggestions for solutions for older school-age children.

2. This chapter is an expansion of this topic in the first and second editions of *Mom's House, Dad's House* (1980, 1997). See "Keeping Children Out of the Middle," pp. 140–143 in the 1997 edition. Also see p. 335 in the 1997 edition and Appendix 2 for research citations and pp. 359–360 for a sample private agreement for managing complaints a child may have about a parent.

CHAPTER

8

Boost Your Skills
for Solving Problems

Steps to Reaching Agreements
Example: The Yearly Time-Share Schedule
Example: Choosing a High School
Your Problem-Solving Style

Coparents spend a lot of time solving problems and untangling situations—from the big questions like how to share time with the children to the everyday ones like the homework left in the other parent's car. Previous chapters had tools for meetings, picking constructive words, and ways to get beyond frustration and those hard feelings. This chapter takes a fresh look at some time-tested tools for solving the bigger issues and making those important decisions that can alter a parent's or a child's life.[1]

The steps to agreements in this chapter are useful tools because they remind us that solving problems takes creativity, negotiation, compromise, listening, and close attention. While these are described in "steps," in real life solving a problem is not that tidy. But if you give these different steps a try, you can have a better chance of either finding a solution or coming up with another way to look at your issue. If you are already doing most, if not all, of these things, then you can use these tools as gentle reminders to yourself.

A sure way of getting the last word in an argument is to say "You're right."

STEPS TO REACHING AGREEMENTS

Before You Begin Discussing Your Issue:

1 **Ask yourself "What" and "Why."** Be crystal clear about your issue, why it is important, and if it fits into your goals. It can actually help to give your issue a name.

2 **Collect information and do research on the subject** and share this information with the other parent before you try to negotiate. Accurate and detailed information is essential to good negotiations.

When You Start Your Discussion:

So True: Hard feelings and sadness can plug up our ears and hide our common sense. Many a good solution has been lost because someone who has treated us badly in the past came up with a good idea before we did. Try to keep an open mind.

3 **Start with "Your View, My View."** Take turns describing the issue as you see it and then your solution or proposal. You don't have to agree but you do need to listen and understand.

- **Your turn:** First, say what is working now, then explain your ideas for solutions, why you think your idea is fair, and how you think your way will work. Give an example. Be sure to explain and show copies of any research or information. Say what you like about the other parent's ideas.

- **Your turn to listen**: First, don't interrupt and listen very carefully. Ask questions, for example: "How would this work?" Ask for any research or other information he or she has.

4 **Play back what you hear about the other person's view. Ask if this is correct**. Keep this up until both of you feel you are understood. Then, it's the other person's turn to listen to you and play back what they heard. Then, you correct them until they are clear about what you said.

5 **Now, talk together about your different ideas.** First, say what you like about the other parent's ideas. Often you can agree on some things about an issue just after listening to each other. For example, parents might agree that their 15-year-old daughter needs to go to summer school, but they don't agree on which classes she takes.

6 **Take out your notepad or computer and write down, right now, where you already agree.** Example: "We agree that our daughter needs to go to summer school." Don't start discussing the classes yet. First, write down where you agree. This step is very important. Don't wait until later.

7 **Talk about where you disagree and brainstorm solutions. Come up with ideas, even unusual ones.**

- Brainstorming means throwing out lots of ideas, even goofy ones.
- For every idea, ask, "How fair is this to our child?" and "If we choose this one, then what might happen?"
- Keep an even tone when you are talking. If you get tense, take a deep breath, and think of CCD. If that's not enough to keep you cool and even-tempered, go to another room or the restroom for just a few minutes and calm down. If that doesn't work, stop the meeting and reschedule.

8 **Pick two or three of the best ideas.** Break these ideas into smaller pieces. There may be one or two of these pieces you can use or a combination of them.

- Try to limit the time you spend in a discussion about one part of an issue. Ten minutes is plenty, less is better. Remember, the longer you spend talking about an issue, the greater the chance that emotions will become more intense.
- Negotiate. Try these tips:

  - **Tradeoffs**—your way with this, my way with that
  - **Compromise**—meet half way
  - **Alternate**—one time with you, one time with me

- Ask yourself, "Is this worth fighting over?" Let little things go.
- Don't drag things out unnecessarily. If you can't decide, say: "I'll think about that and get back to you," and then follow through.
- Don't agree on something during the meeting and then change your mind over the next few days. Better to say you need more time to think about it, and then get back to the other parent. Try not to stall.

The 15-minute rule.

If there are negative feelings lurking around when you are trying to negotiate an agreement, set a 15-minute limit for the meeting. If even during that time it's difficult to manage emotions or to be courteous, first take a break. Walk away for a minute or two. If that doesn't help, even if you have only been talking for 10 minutes, stop the meeting and wait a few days before you try again.

- If your child is old enough, ask for his or her thoughts. While children should not be responsible for making a final decision, they should be heard when the decision is important to them.

9 **Agree on a solution and write it down immediately.**

With the summer school example, Dad wanted his daughter to take algebra again and English. Mom wanted her to take English and a science class. The daughter didn't want to go to school at all. The parents negotiated and decided that their daughter would take English and that she could decide herself whether to take algebra or a science class. They wrote their decision down immediately and in detail. Even waiting a day or two seems to change people's memories at least a little about what they agreed to do.

10 **Finally, look over what you've written, exchange emails later, and fine tune the wording over the next few days.** Then, formally agree to it via email, or you can even print it out and sign it. If your agreement includes a legal matter, then show your final agreement to your attorney.

11 **A few weeks or several months later, ask "Is this solution doing what we hoped it would do?"** Agree on changes if you need them.

Compromise

Monika and Roberto do a good job of coparenting, but like the rest of us they still have their disagreements. Roberto wanted his 8-year-old son Sam to be part of the Pop Warner football team he coaches this year, but Monika said he was still too young to play. They picked up some tips from the steps above and finally agreed that Sam could be part of the football group but that he would be "in training" for next year and not actually play this year. Monika and Roberto did not let the tension about her boyfriend Vern interfere with decisions about the children.

EXAMPLE:
THE YEARLY TIME-SHARE SCHEDULE

The Problem to Solve: The What and Why

Here's an example of parents who have a section in their Parenting Plan that says they meet every February to design a year's schedule. This schedule goes from June to June and includes the school year, three-day holidays, summer school, camps, December holidays, and Spring Breaks. They want to finish the schedule by the end of February so everyone can make summer plans. Their goal is a schedule that is fair and easy on their 10 and 5-year-old sons. The oldest boy has been spending 30%–35% of the time with his father and the youngest stays with Mom about 75% of the time.

Collect Information

They have nearly all the information they think they need. They find out later that an important piece is missing.

Start the Discussion with Your View/My View

Mom talks first about what she thinks has worked well this past year and then lays out her ideas for the master schedule. Dad listens, then *asks specific questions* about dates, times, transportation. He doesn't jump in to say what he disagrees with.

Play Back What You Hear

Ask if this is correct. Dad repeats back to Mom what he thinks she's saying. She corrects a few points here and there. Then it's Dad's turn to talk, and Mom tells him what she heard him say and Dad corrects her. By this time they both have a good idea where they agree and disagree. They have each had their say and feel heard. It is very important that people feel you really listened and understood. If the playback part is missing, this may not happen.

Then Talk about Each Other's Ideas

They see that their consistent attention and work over the past few years has paid off and that their current schedule is working well. They agree

We learned early in the divorce process that we would rather keep the money for ourselves and our children than spend the money in court because we couldn't agree on our own.

—A coparent Dad

YOUR IDEAS

to continue nearly all of it but make a few changes about the times Dad picks up the 5-year-old after school and his days with him.

Write Detailed Notes

Write down your areas of agreement. Clear up some details. Mom has her laptop and she types in their agreements. Later, she will send the file to Dad for review and corrections or additions. They will email it back and forth until they are satisfied with it.

Talk about Disagreements

Take one issue at a time. Their only major disagreement is over Mom's proposal that she has two extra days at Christmas again this year so she can take a trip with the kids.

Missing information. Because the parents had already collected all the schedule information for the schools, certain sports, and outside activities, they were able to almost finish the calendar. But Mom doesn't have the departure and arrival times for her proposed trip. Since she doesn't have that information, they end their meeting and decide to take this up later. Besides, Dad wants to think more about Mom's request.

Brainstorm Solutions

A few days later, Mom emails Dad the trip information and exact departure times. Mom explains the travel restrictions that require the extra time. However, Dad's position now is that he gave Mom two days last year for another trip and he is unwilling to give up two days again. They brainstorm and come up with different options for trading times, dividing days, and tradeoffs. They even thought about just flipping a coin. They narrow down the best ideas and then ask, "If we went with this option, how might this play out?"

Agree on a Solution

They agree to trade some days: Mom will have the two extra days before Christmas that she wants and Dad will now have three extra days for Spring Break.

Write Out the Agreement

This time, Dad writes out the agreement, adds it to the first agreements they wrote out earlier, and sends the full draft of the yearly schedule to Mom for her review. After exchanging some emails on details, they finally agree on everything and finalize it.

Look at How the Solution Is Working

Three weeks after the new schedule begins in June, they talk again. They have to make a slight adjustment to accommodate a summer camp, but otherwise it looks good.

> *Question:* What if the situation is life-changing, like moving away or choosing a school? Do we use the same steps?
>
> *Answer:* Yes, but before you even try and reach agreement, both of you should do a full investigation. Do more than asking others about it or researching on the internet. Go in person and together if you can. Go to the schools or the new city, get a feel for it, and talk to people there. Combine your personal experience and the data collected. See the next example.

EXAMPLE: CHOOSING A HIGH SCHOOL

Selecting a high school is one of the most important decisions parents make. If parents get off course by skipping the research step, they will not have important information. This can tangle up the discussions, delay action, and change the course of the decision. Here is an example where parents don't agree on which high school their 13-year-old boy, Kai, will attend next Fall. It is late October and Kai is in his last year of middle school. When they do get around to getting the information they need to make such a decision, they find out much more than they expected.

Kai's Issues

Kai was getting Bs last year, but now his mother has found at least three papers with Ds. He isn't seeing his friends anymore. He just stays in his room and plays electronic games online. Kai says he is bullied at school and doesn't want to go at all. Mom thinks Kai is depressed, Dad thinks these are just excuses to not do the work. Mom wants Kai to go to the public high school next year where she thinks there are many resources for him, while Dad wants him to go to a private school nearby where the teachers will make him do the work. The parents do not listen to each other's views, and their discussions disintegrate into arguments. To make matters worse, neither of them had collected information from teachers about what is actually happening to Kai this semester or official information about the two possible high schools. The parents' views are coming from their own observations and opinions collected from friends.

The "Research"

Finally, Dad decides to talk with Kai's teachers, expecting to be reassured that Kai is just goofing off. Instead, he finds that the teachers believe that Kai has serious issues. They say Kai doesn't concentrate, won't participate in class, and has skipped class more and more. Two teachers say they heard that he was being harassed on a social network site and with some texting but couldn't confirm this. They also said that they worried that Kai was slipping into a depression. Dad is alarmed and tells Mom what he's found. The Vice-Principal sets up a meeting for the parents with the school counselor for the next day.

    The counselor understands their shock and concerns. He knows that things like this happen in many families and he urges them to take several steps right away. First, set limits on Kai's use of his electronics until he pulls up his grades, second, hire a tutor to help Kai catch up, third, provide Kai with personal counseling with an expert in teen behavior, and fourth, either work with the teen counselor on parenting approaches or see their own counselor to put together the united front Kai needs. The counselor strongly suggests that when they are ready they tell Kai about his options for high school. The counselor recommended that Kai visit these local schools with them soon. Dad is relieved that they have a clear set of action steps to take and that the teen counselor is on their health insurance. Mom is feeling ashamed that she didn't check with the school earlier but feels hopeful that they can turn things around. To their credit, Mom and Dad start working as a team. Dad doesn't criticize Mom for not following through at school sooner, and Mom doesn't say "I told you so" to Dad about Kai's depression. Good for them. Time to move on to solve the problem at hand.

Action

The parents talk to Kai together about Dad's visit to the school and tell him that they will support him to do better in school and want him to be happier. Kai is comforted by the fact his parents seem to be in agreement and not arguing. He does not resist the idea of a teen counselor and he seems relieved about the tutor. He is not happy about the strict limits on his gaming and social networking though. He also learns that all the adults will be in contact with each other about his progress. The parents will talk about the cyberbullying issue with the counselor and Kai together.

Pull Together Different Options—Brainstorm

Once Kai was settling into his new routine, his parents turn their attention to choosing a high school for next year. After much discussion and considering possible consequences, the parents look at the following options: home schooling, sending him to live with his aunt and uncle, a boarding school, public high school, or the private high school. They decide they want Kai to stay there with them.

They visit the two local high schools (public and private) and ask many questions about their resources and policies on bullying. The parents find that the private school only accepts students with a B- or higher average their last two years in middle school who were involved in at least one activity. The public high school does not have these restrictions. The parents then talk to Kai about high schools and explain the different options they had considered. They tell him that they definitely want things to work out so he can keep living with them and go to one of the local high schools.

Kai then goes to visit each of the high schools with his parents. He is clear that his first choice is the private school. He knows he has to get at least a B- average and start an activity now. His parents tell him they will support his choice. If he is not accepted into the private school, the parents explain that they still want him to maintain that B- average and have a school activity in the public high school. If he is unable to do that, the last resort is for him to go live with his aunt and uncle who live 200 miles away in a highly regarded school district with an outstanding high school. The principal is his aunt's brother.

The parents write down what Kai has to do and why. Kai adds his own views. Because Kai is old enough, they make it all into a contract which Kai signs. After Kai has been in counseling, has joined an activity, and has had tutoring for several months, the parents and Kai will talk about his progress. Next school year, if Kai does get into the private school, the parents will evaluate the situation after the first semester. Then they'll decide whether he should continue there.

The choice of high schools for Kai was a complicated process because, instead of one decision, there were important decisions to be made before choosing a specific school. This family was successful because the parents came together to work as a team, checked out information personally, came up with their options, chose their best ones, and then brought in their teenager to be part of the final decisions. Now Kai has some ownership in decisions that directly affect him in a possible life-changing way.

well done

> **Question:** What if we did do all that research and still couldn't agree on most things? What if the other parent is saying, "It's my way or the highway."
>
> **Answer:** If there is no a real give and take, then it's time to get a neutral third party like a mediator or a coparenting counselor to help you get some balance in your relationship and decisionmaking. If that doesn't work, then it's possible that coparenting may not work. An experienced counselor can help you sort this out.

YOUR PROBLEM-SOLVING STYLE

How did you make decisions and solve disagreements when you were living together? If you had a reasonably successful system, then you are well on your way as coparents. If you were only a little successful, then here are some thoughts on different ways people act when there's a problem to solve.

What's Your Style?

Maybe you want to pick up your child an hour earlier, or you think the other parent is not following your agreement. What do you say and how do you say it? Does your style get you what you want or at least something you are willing to live with? It helps some parents to label problem-solving styles when trying to solve a problem. Even though people seem to use a combination of the following approaches, some people still have a "go-to" style when they are pushed to the wall. Look at these styles and ask yourself: What combination of styles do you use and what combination does your coparent seem to use?

The Situation. Lynne is a mom whose parents are coming into town next month the same weekend the children are with their father, John. Lynne wants John to let the children stay with her so they can spend as much time with the grandparents as possible. Although Lynne and John have been flexible about this type of request in the past, John is unhappy with Lynne's refusal to consider his proposal that he have the children half time and Lynne knows it. How will she approach John? What is her usual style?

The Teddy Bear **"Be Nice," accommodate, don't make waves**. The Teddy Bear style is easy to be with, makes no demands, and might actually ignore the whole situation until it's too late. This person just wants people to be happy. It's easy for others to dismiss or take advantage of a person with this style. If Lynne's usual style is that of the Teddy Bear, she would tentatively ask her parents to change their plans, and when they say they can't, she asks John about the weekend. John says he is not willing to give up that time. Lynne says, "OK, I just thought I would ask," and doesn't try to change his mind. She knows her children and her parents will be disappointed. She feels defeated. Some fathers would want their children to see their grandparents and suggest they trade some days. But John knows it's easy to get his way just by refusing. Lynne's resentments build each time John is inflexible. Down the road, Lynne may change her style but she won't forget John's inflexibility. If the situation were reversed and you were trying to negotiate with a person who prefers to take the Teddy Bear approach, it's wiser to discuss the situation in detail and ask for his or her ideas on how to reach a compromise. Move slowly. Teddy Bears can keep score.

The Rabbit **"I'll ignore it or just run and hide."** The Rabbit is easily spooked. When a person prefers this style, they are easily upset or threatened. They may avoid the issue, "forget" like the Teddy Bear, freeze, or run away from it. They can't seem to take action. If Lynne was a person who preferred this style, it may not occur to her to ask her parents to adjust their plans so they are there on the days the children are with her. She might not get around to asking John until it's too late and John has already made other plans for the children. Or she tells him the situation but doesn't think ahead to offer him an alternative. If you are trying to negotiate with a person who often acts like a Rabbit, just as with the Teddy Bear move slowly and in steps. Present your request and give reassuring details. Ask for his or her thoughts and suggest several options. If you must have an answer right away, at least give him or her a day or so to think about it. Then return for an answer. Usually, don't expect a quick decision but do expect that the person may change their mind a time or two.

The Bull **"My way is the only way."** The Bull is strong, is action-oriented, gets things done, is assertive, and a leader. The Bull wants it done now. This approach is the most competitive. When winning is most important, the Bull is overly aggressive and uses threats or bullies. If Lynne prefers this style, she may tell her parents their timing is not good and that they should come on her weekend instead. Or, she doesn't ask John what he wants but just tells him she's keeping the kids that weekend. If John refused, Lynne could dig in her heels and argue with him. If John acted like a Bull himself and got angry back at her, she could retaliate and make threats like calling her attorney. People who lose arguments with the heavy-handed "Bulls" can become resentful. These resentments pile up. The best way to deal with a Bull is to explain the situation, and then suggest options where things are evenly divided and he or she still retains control of one portion. In this case, Lynne might have offered to divide that particular weekend between them and to have a trade day during the upcoming week or the following weekend to make up for the one day she is taking from his weekend with the kids.

The Dolphin **"We're a Team," "We problem-solve and collaborate**." The "Dolphin" is very aware of how one action or person affects another and tries to solve the problem by including everyone involved. If Lynne prefers this approach, she would first ask the grandparents to change their plans, and when they cannot, she explains the grandparents' travel plans to John. She gives him plenty of notice. She asks him for his ideas on alternatives so the girls can spend time with their grandparents. John says that even if he traded that weekend, he would not have the children overnight for another two weeks and that this is not fair to either him or the children. The parents then discuss alternatives such as extra overnights the next week, an extended weekend, just one day instead of both days. Lynne calls the grandparents about some modifications, and together they all find a plan that solves the problem. John says he wants the children to have a close relationship with their grandparents. Lynne tells John she has a better appreciation of how important it is that he has more time with the children. She also says she would like to explore ways to change the schedule so that could happen. Both want their future discussions to be more like this one where they explore the situation in more depth. A lot got done with this negotiation. Good will all around.

Combination of Styles

While these four styles can help explain some things about how people go about considering changes and making decisions, these are just useful categories. In real life, everyone approaches discussions somewhat differently depending on the situation. Rarely are people boxed in with just one way. For example, Kai's Dad sometimes did some things like a Bull, but other times as a Dolphin. Kai's Mom seemed to take on some of the habits of a Teddy Bear, but at times also of a Bull and a Dolphin. Notice that they became a team by revising their opinions after getting key information. When people take the time to examine and understand a situation, listen respectfully to one another and ask questions, solutions often fall naturally into place.

When people take the time to examine and understand a situation, listen respectfully to one another and ask questions, solutions often fall naturally into place.

NOTE FOR CHAPTER 8

1. *Mom's House, Dad's House for KIDS* also has several different ways kids themselves can solve disagreements and problems. See pp. 103–120, "You Can Become an Ace Problem Solver."

Find Ways to Help Your Child

Things Kids Want Parents to Know
What Parents Can Do to Help Their Child
Going Back and Forth between Homes
House and Safety Rules
What Do You Want for Your Child?

Coparenting is parenting with a Plus. The up-tick doesn't have to be dramatic, but kids need parents to pay a little more attention, be more patient, observant, and available. This is especially true the months before, during, and after the separation when changes can lead to problems in the best of circumstances. Remember, kids have more things going on inside themselves even when they don't show it on the outside. Children often have fears of being abandoned, hurt, unloved, unimportant, losing friends, their school, their use of the family car, ability to participate in a sport, or funding for a college education. Parents can work together to give their children this extra attention now. This can assure children that things will eventually work out well.

The "Plus" for you as a coparent is pulling together your own combination of what your children want and need, what you already know how to do, and what more you can actually do as a new parenting team. Keep your eyes open for signs that things are not working well but continue to enjoy your daily life as a family.

Take a look at what kids want parents to know. You will see some repeats of guidelines and suggestions on this list from earlier chapters. This is so you can have these all in one place.

THINGS KIDS
WANT PARENTS TO KNOW[1]

put kids first

1   We need to know you love us, will protect us, and won't leave us. *Underneath we are scared and confused.* We need to hear that you will see that things will work out. *Be here more. Hug us more.*

2   Show us it's OK to love both of you. Don't tell us ugly things about our other parent. Act respectful to each other when we're around.

3   Tell us that we aren't to blame for your problems and that we shouldn't try to fix them. *Be careful what adult things you tell us. We aren't adults no matter how we act or what we say. Confide in people your own age. We can't be your "best" friend or spouse.*

4   Accept that we need a lot of time to adjust even when we don't show it. Give us space and time to grieve the loss of our old life at our own pace.

5   Please listen respectfully to our feelings and questions even when you don't agree or do anything about them. Help us express our feelings and coach us on how to manage them.[2]

6   Keep your arguments to yourself. We really shouldn't see them, hear about them, or get in the middle of your stuff with the other parent. We are just kids. *Especially, don't ask us to spy, pass messages, or take sides.*

7   Don't stress us out with way different rules at each house like punishments, bedtimes, curfews, or homework. Please remember that keeping all this straight is not easy, no matter what we say.

8   Help us get organized for going back and forth and be calm and patient about it.

9   Please make it easy for us to go to our other parent. Show us it's okay to be there. You can miss us but don't make us feel guilty for going or for being happy to see our other parent.

10   We want both of you to know about our schoolwork, activities, friends, hopes, what scares us, what makes us happy and confident.

11 Give us a chance to talk with kids who are also going through this. Read or talk with us about books on divorce so we know what to expect.

If you can do these things, it would help us a lot.

WHAT PARENTS CAN DO
TO HELP THEIR CHILD[3]

- Show your children that you will always be there for them and take care of them. Give more hugs, touches, cuddles. Say more "I love you," "I'll always take care of you."
- Be there in person as much as possible.
- Know their strengths and find ways to acknowledge and support them.
- Give your child your full attention. Listen well.[4]
- When you are not together, be in contact more with phone calls, texts, emails.
- Spend more quality time doing projects or activities together and teaching life skills.
- Protect your child from your adult arguments and issues. This can't be said often enough.
- Keep order and structure with routines, eating meals together, house rules, and insistence on mutual respect. Again, this is worth repeating.
- Memorize the list Things Kids Want Parents to Know in this chapter.
- Be happy with your child! Make family work and homework more enjoyable. Try to do things where you can have fun at the same time.

Our way of being a family has changed, but we are still a real family. We can have a good future.
—A Mom

GOING BACK AND FORTH BETWEEN HOMES
Make it low stress for everyone!

Picking Up and Dropping Off

Parents try different systems for making the transition of their children from one parent to the other. Here are a few routines people use. Just be sure whatever you try, that it is as low stress as possible.[5]

1. **School-week transition.** The current resident parent brings the child to school. The other parent picks the child up after school.

2. **An afterschool or weekend activity transition.** The current resident parent sees that the child goes to the activity and stays there until the other parent arrives to pick up the child for their time together.

3. **Other transition days. The resident parent brings the child to the other parent.** This seems to help some children understand that it is okay to go to the other parent if the other parent brings them. Also, this avoids the situation of a parent waiting for a child to be ready or a child waiting for the parent to arrive.

4. **The "receiving" parent comes to the resident parent's home.** If a parent must pick up a child at the other home, then decide together what the routine will be. Will the parent wait by the curb or driveway or come to the door? If it's the door, then decide on what to do about that awkward period. The rule is that a parent doesn't come into the other parent's home without being invited in. Does a parent wait on the doorstep or come into the house? If it's in the house, where?

Remedies for Stressful Transitions

If getting ready and then bringing your child to the other parent are too stressful for you, you can bet it's stressful for your child. A child can get anxious and worried that they'll forget something and then get yelled at. Or, they can get upset because the pet they leave behind will miss them or that one parent doesn't want them to leave. A big problem mentioned in earlier chapters is where angry or upset parents meet face-to-face. Children might dread the transition time because they fear their parents might hurt each other's feelings, argue, be sarcastic, or shoot each other dirty looks. This can be very painful for your child.

If you have this stressful situation, try to transition from one home to the other where you do not speak directly to each other and can just wave to each other as you see your child go to the protection of the other parent. If you have teenagers who are licensed, can drive safely, and your homes are close together, the teen can transport the other children. If not, try the school-week transition. The goal is to protect the children from a painful situation and give them a whole school day where they can just be themselves before they transition from one home and one parent to the other. The typical pattern is that on the transition day, a parent brings the child to school. Then the receiving parent picks up the child after school. If the child has extra bags or equipment, parents get creative with ways those things can also transfer. Many schools have provisions for this. Do try to avoid late-evening transitions in empty parking lots where children walk alone from one car to the other, or where they don't get to bed until late.

Find your best "transition" situation, one where your child does not feel stress, his or her routine is not particularly interrupted, they get a balanced meal, and where he or she can feel that going with the other parent is okay with you and you are going to be just fine. Some kids may actually say, "Promise?" And hopefully, you will reassure them and answer, "Yes."

"What Am I Supposed to Do? I Forgot."

Children can also feel anxious going back and forth because they are supposed to remember many different things. No one likes to feel confused or inadequate because things are changing. So here are some tips to consider.

Help Your Child Remember These 4 Things[6]

1. Where they are going.
2. How they get there and what time they get picked up.
3. How they get back and when they get picked up, where, by whom.
4. What stuff they need to bring with them.

Think Routine

Routines mean you have a system you don't have to continually reinvent or argue about. Think about having a routine for the day before and the day when the children transition to the other parent. Perhaps it's a reminder the night before, a time when you help them get things together, or a conversation about pets that need care while they are away, a place by the door for all their things that transfer, or a checklist you and the kids use. Try out different ways and then pick one that works for now. As kids grow older, the routine will probably change.

Re-Entry

Changing homes, beds, and parents requires a "re-entry" process. Kids need a "settling in" and re-orientation time when they arrive at the other home. Everyone—parents and kids—have their own style of re-entry.[7] In *Mom's House, Dad's House for Kids: Feeling at Home in One Home or Two*, pages 72–73, there are examples of different re-entry styles, including ways to avoid a blowup. When parents understand a child's style and adjust their expectations, things can be easier all around. For example, a Dad understands that his daughter doesn't want to talk much when he picks her up from school. When they get to the house, she just wants to get physically reoriented and wants to do it without adults, thank you very much. She quietly grabs a snack and she's off to the room she shares with her older stepsister. Dad and stepmom have learned to back off and that they will see her at dinner when she's more settled in. This girl has one style but other children handle re-entry differently. Let your children guide you toward the "re-entry" process that helps them to settle in.

HOUSE AND SAFETY RULES

Structure feels safe, and house and safety rules can be the mainstay for rebuilding basic trust

House Rules. Structure feels safe and house and safety rules can be the mainstay for rebuilding basic trust. Rules are an essential part of any family structure, and when expectations are clear it also shows children that their parent is their leader and in charge. Rules are also the way the family team pulls together and the way children learn about values and responsibility. Rules are not just "Do as I say", but a way for a child to develop self-confidence, a sense of importance, as well as life skills. For parents who already have these rules, separation and divorce are times when it's a good idea to revisit them and refresh them for everyone. Rules can be short or long and can be about things like the way the family treats the house, yard, pets, property, food, and guests.

You can set out rules for bedtimes, meals, homework, electronics, friends, purchases, computers, the Internet, anything you like, even allowances and food choices. Every child, including teens, needs structure, rules, and limits. Within these boundaries, they can be free to test, be creative, and learn. When Mom and Dad have many (or all) of the same rules, it's a relief to the children. Different rules are not easy to keep straight. When a child forgets (and they are just children, after all), then parents get upset. It's not fair to the children.

It's easier for a child to hear, "Your dirty clothes are still on the floor. You know the Rules." This makes it something that they are to do because they are a member of the family and have a responsibility to the family. If you say, "Go pick up your dirty clothes," or worse, "Go pick up your dirty clothes for me," it can sound like the picking up the clothes is your responsibility instead of theirs. If you don't already have your own house rules, *Appendix 4: House Rules* has a sample form to get you started.

Safety Rules. Safety Rules are straightforward. "You must always wear a helmet when you ride your bike," for example. As children grow, parents teach children about certain situations and people, about risks from equipment and appliances. But even though you think your children have these rules clear in their minds, it may also be good to write out some of the ones you feel are the most important. You might have more worries about heaters, furnaces/air conditioners, stoves, in the car, on bikes, skates, skis, using certain equipment, or house security. Add whatever you want on your list. Try to have a family talk with everyone where the kids can themselves list their own safety rules. This will also show you which ones they forget. Have you recently moved to a new place? Then going over safety rules for this home and this neighborhood is an important step to do now.[8]

Safety with electronics and the Internet. In order for parents to help protect their children from unsafe and unwise uses of phones, texting, social networking, blogs, and other Internet and electronics resources, parents must keep up to date. New challenges seem to come up every week, and simply blocking websites from your child's computer will not be enough. Research shows that children find ways to do things on the Internet that they don't want their parents to know about. It's especially shocking to find that one out of every five children is solicited online by sexual predators. *Appendix 3: Safety Rules* has more on what parents can do about this.

Safety and security numbers need to be posted where the children can see and use them if necessary. *Appendix 8: Important Phone Numbers, Safety and Emergency Hotlines* has a sample form to get you started.

Same or Different Rules in Both Homes

Try to keep bedtimes, mealtimes, homework expectations, and curfews the same or nearly the same at each home. Realistically, even never-separated parents disagree on certain things, but most people realize it's healthier to present a united front or to respectfully disagree without expecting the child to take a side. So, if you disagree on bedtime or mealtimes, talk it out. And find a way to support each other's point of view with the child and the rules of each home.[9]

YOUR IDEAS

Discipline in Both Homes

Discipline from one home should be carried over to the other home whenever possible. Mitchell, age 15, has been smoking pot. His grades have gone down and he has a bad attitude. His Dad has grounded him until he brings his grades up and he can honestly promise to stay smoke-free. Mitchell was used to going out with his older friends on weekends. Mom feels Dad's discipline is too harsh, and Mitchell pressures her to let him go out on Saturday with his friends. How would you handle this as a coparent team? What would Mitchell learn?

Daily Life

The kids' activities and social life. In this book, there are frequent reminders to keep each other informed about the children and their activities. Now add this. Even if the other parent doesn't legally share decision making with you, give him or her a chance to have input into your decisions. It can make for a better working relationship.

Toys, electronics, Internet, games, cars, and bikes. Coparents are both blessed and challenged today by the many ways we can communicate, play, socialize, and exercise. Coparents can put their heads together and decide what's fair and what's safe and healthy. They should also keep an eye open for research that is beginning to suggest that certain electronics may pose a risk to a child's brain development and health.

Last-Minute Changes—Everyone Needs to Get the Same Message. Cell phone calling and texting, even tweeting, can be a coparent's best friend. But, it only works if the child's phone is charged, not left behind, or lost, and the child actually reads and answers a parent's message. Just try to see that everyone gets the same information. In the crush of daily life, it's easy to forget to tell a child or the other parent important details. Confirm and then be confident.

Playing One Parent Against the Other

Kids naturally try to play a parent against the other to get their way. They may do more of this after separation, especially if they think the parents aren't communicating well. They are just being kids, but if you check things out with each other as suggested in *Chapter 6: Try These Tools to Side-Step Communication Potholes*, it sends them a message that their parents do keep in touch about them and can still pick up on their games.

When Rules Get Complicated.

Cody's girlfriend Hanna thinks that since Cody and the kids are living in her house, the children should follow her house rules—which are quite different from Laura's and what the parents had when they were married. The younger kids are now telling their Mom they don't want to go to Dad's and complain about Hanna. Hanna is doing her best and she is hurt, Laura is angry, and Cody hates being in the middle. When a parent starts living with a new partner, especially if it is because of an affair during the marriage, everyone—the three adults and the children—all have an especially challenging road to travel. Laura and Cody are now doing better managing their tone and behavior in front of the children. Their emails and texts are more business-like and CCD. However, competing House Rules are a problem, especially for Megan. Privately, when Laura thinks about another woman taking a parent role with her children, it makes her feel crazy. Cody doesn't know what to do. He sympathizes with Hanna, but he also knows that his daughter Megan needs consistency and believes that Laura is so set in her ways that it will take months before she compromises. For her part, Hanna is rethinking the wisdom of living with a man who has three children and a "My way or the highway" former wife. It's complicated.

Rules Between Homes

Consistent house and safety rules are a big part of helping children adjust to two homes.

WHAT DO YOU WANT FOR YOUR CHILD?

Look ahead to a time when your child is 24–25 years old. What values, attitudes, and behaviors would you hope your child had developed? Look at this beginning list, add your own, and then circle the top 10–15. If you have very young children, narrow it down further to just 2 or 3 for now. You and the other parent don't have to agree on these. Just get started thinking more specifically about what you hope for.

loving, gentle, strong, high self-esteem, self-confident, resilient, persistent, kind, thoughtful, polite, respectful, hard-working, good judgment, curious, adventuresome, practical, creative, team player, supportive, protective, honest, problem-solver, resourceful, trustworthy, perceptive, courteous, kind, in touch with own feelings, practical, good with people, socially aware, fun-loving, ambitious, relaxed (Write in your own below.)

_____

_____

_____

How Will Your Child Learn These Values and Traits?

Even if our children don't show it, they are usually watching us to see what we think is important by the decisions we make, our attitudes, and how we treat others. We are our children's first and most important teacher. Ask yourself—

How will they learn a certain trait or embrace a value?

◯ from my example?

◯ from my explanations and stories?

◯ from my pointing out how other people act?

◯ from the Internet, TV, movies, their friends, other adults, what they learn in school?

Patience—A Few Examples

Dad patiently waits while the 3-year-old buttons his shirt and then explains to the 6-year-old that everyone waited patiently for him when he was little, too. Mom tells her teenager that she admires the math teacher because she is patient and helps students think through a solution without getting cranky.

Honesty—A Few Examples

Dad doesn't brag about cheating on his taxes or getting away with exceeding the speed limit. Mom doesn't say, "Don't let me catch you doing this . . ." because that means if you are dishonest and don't get caught, it's okay to do that dishonest thing. Mom explains to James that calling her sister "Fatty" (even though sister is overweight) is not being "honest." James is using what he calls "honesty" to hurt his sister's feelings. Frieda tells her Dad the truth about why she was late getting home from the park. Dad tells Frieda that her honesty is one of the reasons he can trust her with the car.

Hard Work and Effort—A Few Examples

Dad works hard and talks about how good it feels to do his best. Mom is upbeat about learning a new language, "I've been sticking with it and I'm finally seeing some real progress." Dad tells his 8-year-old he's impressed with his effort at keeping his room neater. Mom cooks three days of meals for the family on Saturdays so that when she comes in from work the next week, it will be easier for them all to have a hot supper earlier. She would rather sit and read a book on a Saturday, but her family's needs come first.

well done

Your Own Values Worksheet

VALUE, TRAIT	I AM A ROLE MODEL BY . . .	OTHERS WHO MODEL THIS . . .

Question: One of the reasons I left my partner last year is because everything had to be about her and her needs. Now my 14-year-old son says that his mother is "So into herself, she doesn't even listen when I tell her about my problems with the math teacher or this girl I like." He's disgusted with her. What do I say?

Answer: This is a very important question. Please do not encourage your son's negative beliefs and disrespectful attitude toward his mother, no matter how much you might agree with him. Children can sense when a parent doesn't especially like the other parent and this can give some teenagers a sense that they can talk trash about that parent. This disrespect undermines the other parent's authority, and while you may get some points with your son about this now, it doesn't pay off for you or for him down the road.

You can ask him to describe the situation for you in calmer tones—especially what he wanted Mom to hear about school and this girl. Point out that even when he is upset with his mother, he needs be respectful. Then, you can tell him gently but firmly that he needs to tell her in person that he needs her to listen to what he says and to take it seriously. Aside from your advice, this can also be a good life lesson for your son. Everyone has personality traits that may or may not change (even when we wish they would) and people, including parents, are not perfect. Over time, we learn to accept others as they are. Encourage your child to keep trying to talk with the other parent and to do so with respect.[9]

NOTES FOR CHAPTER 9

1. Things Kids Want Parents to Know, is adapted from "Divorce from the Kids' Point of View" by Isolina Ricci, *NCFR Report*, December 2007.

2. For an inside look at what children need, their emotions and questions for parents, see *Mom's House, Dad's House for KIDS*, pp. 7–35.

3. *Mom's House, Dad's House*, pp. 133–154, goes into detail about how to promote security and continuity for your child.

4. See *Mom's House, Dad's House for KIDS* for more examples of how difficult it is for children to express themselves and for the "Words to Try" section. Start on p. 37.

5. In *Mom's House, Dad's House for KIDS*, Part I, Divorce Territory, there are many tips that parents themselves can use to help their child make the transitions and help organize their new schedule, especially pp. 68–75.

6. Adapted from *Mom's House, Dad's House for KIDS*, p. 56.

7. In *Mom's House, Dad's House for KIDS*, pp. 72–73, there are several "re-entry" styles described.

8. See *Mom's House, Dad's House*, pp. 118-122, for more information.

9. Page 67 in *Mom's House, Dad's House for KIDS* talks about "New Rules, Old Rules, Confusing Rules."

10. In *Mom's House, Dad's House*, p. 134, there is a further explanation about what affects children, including the impact of the family's history before the separation.

CHAPTER

10

Fine Tune Your Parenting Style

Consider Your Parenting Style
Guidelines for the Developmental Parenting Style
Your Child's Temperament and Moving
Parenting Checklist

CONSIDER YOUR PARENTING STYLE

When it comes to parenting, there's no such thing as a one-size-fits-all approach. But some things are universal. We love our children. We want to watch them grow and be all they can be. We want our children to be able to live satisfying and honorable lives. How can parents help them thrive in today's world with its many different cultures and a competitive global economy? How can they help their children be prepared?

Parenting is a challenge for everyone, so give your coparent a break.

Experts have suggested various parenting styles based on theory, research, observation, and personal experience. Often they classify general styles. As parents, we might use one style more than another, but we probably use combinations according to the situation. Read about these four styles below to refresh what you know and perhaps find some new information.[1]

Four Common Styles of Parenting

- **Authoritarian** "My way or the highway."
- **Permissive** "Children rule. Parents obey."
- **Not Involved** Children are not a priority.
- **Developmental** "We're a team. Parents are the leaders."

The Authoritarian Parent—"My way or the highway." This is probably the most familiar style. It has been used throughout the ages, and may seem easiest even if it's not effective in the long term. The parent has all the control and authority and makes all the decisions no matter how old the child is. A parent may believe that this level of control is the best way to express their love and protection. In its extreme form, the authoritarian parent expects unquestioning obedience to orders.[2]

This style can be overly protective but does set high standards and expects achievement. Even though the parent may deeply love the child, the parent does not encourage discussion or disagreements. The rules are usually clear and consistent but there is little room for new information or new circumstances. If extreme, punishment can be harsh and may include spanking, threats, and forms of bullying. Unfortunately, even though a parent may be devoted, this parenting style can raise children who either rebel and distance themselves from the parent or are angry and oppositional. In contrast, they might become young adults who are unable to think on their own and are easily led into harmful situations by another authoritarian or strong personality. In today's complex society, children need to gradually learn how to make their own good judgments about people and situations. They must manage competing values and opportunities. A parent cannot be constantly at their side making these decisions for them.

Permissive or Indulgent Parenting—"Children rule. Parents obey." This style of parenting is the flip side of the authoritarian style. Parents may be warm, sensitive, and supportive of the child, but they exert very little control. They take a back seat, assuming that children can learn from the consequences of their actions without guidance or boundaries. The parents do not want to be disliked or to see unhappy children and may treat the child as a best friend, an equal, or as their boss. Children may not be taught to value limits or the rights of others, so children can assume they have the same rights as adults and may become overly demanding with an overdose of entitlement. Parents may not set clear limits or coach their child in behaviors that would help them integrate into groups or into a structured school or work situation. When a child is irresponsible or behaves badly, the parent may feel powerless to do anything or ignores or justifies the behavior.

Often, permissive parents do not set expectations for achievement or social behavior as do the authoritarian and developmental parents. Although children raised in this style may be creative and original, they often have poor social skills, have trouble taking responsibility for others, and lack understanding of the consequences of their behaviors. Unfortunately, children may lack appreciation of other people's rights and can become overly aggressive when frustrated. There may also be

---

A "Warm" Parent gives soft hugs, pats, touches, smiles, cuddles, makes loving eye-contact, shows genuine interest in a child's feelings, uses a kind voice tone and sweet words of encouragement. This can happen at any time and is spontaneous and automatic. Parents often have positive nicknames for their children and use endearments like "honey," "sweetheart," "big guy." **A "Sensitive" Parent** picks up on a child's needs, interests, feelings, fears, and engages the child in conversation and activities. The child feels cherished, important, and understood.

situations where they may become passive and vulnerable to feeling victimized. They may feel confused, insecure, and have difficulty making good choices. In permissive families, the members may just go their own way with no sense of responsibility to one another or to family ties.

Noninvolved Parenting—"Children are not a priority." This parenting style is not really parenting. Parents may be emotionally distracted, oblivious, or rejecting of their child's needs. Some noninvolved parents are actually neglectful to the point where their children do lack proper nourishment, sleep, or a clean place to live. But, there are others who do give their children clothing, shelter, advantages money can buy, but they are not actively or lovingly involved in the child's life. The parent may keep the child busy with activities, friends, lessons, or computer/video games, but the parents are emotionally unavailable, often lack warmth, and are more invested in their adult activities or their work. They do not have an ongoing interest in their child's inner life and dreams. The child can feel adrift because the parent is not connected to them in a meaningful way. When these children become adults, the parent might say, "I don't understand why they aren't happy and successful (or don't keep in contact). I gave them the best of everything."

The Better Choice—Developmental Parenting

If you have surfed the Web for books and articles on parenting styles, you know that there is one general style, often called either "democratic," "assertive," or "authoritative" (not authoritarian) that is more likely to give your child the self-confidence and tools to do well in today's world. The "developmental parenting" style here is an adaption of these similar styles.

To begin with, a developmental parent is warm, sensitive, and responsive to the child and makes sure there is a strong bond between them. This parent learns to appreciate a child's limits based on the child's age and development—physically, emotionally, and intellectually. With developmental parenting, the parent sets limits as the undisputed family leader, is on top of things, knows where the kids are and what they are doing, and has the final word. The child feels secure and loved.

This is the style that makes kids accountable but is also respectful of them as individuals. This parent involves the children in discussions about decisions and is on his or her toes, protecting, nurturing, teaching, coaching, and supporting.[3] A developmental parent is warm and loving, and while there's lots of time spent together, a parent does not use the child as a "best friend" or confidant. Parents who have this style raise children

What Is Basic Trust and Why Does a Child Need It?

A child's sense of basic trust is based on the feeling that life is predictable, safe, and good, that his or her needs will be met, that he or she is loved, valued, and protected. There's a belief that if things don't work out today, there is always tomorrow. When parents separate or divorce, a child's "basic trust" can be severely tested and shaken. Good, sensitive parenting and coparenting can rebuild your child's basic trust.

"We're a family team. Parents are the leaders and have the final word."

who can accept responsibility, be self-reliant, respect adults and authority, be creative, read other people, and know him or herself. They have been raised to make good choices, be members of teams, keep jobs, and cope with change and challenges without blind reliance on or automatic rebellion toward a leader or an authority. This style has the potential of giving children the best tools and self-confidence for today's multidimensional world with its many choices and different cultural perspectives.

> Parenting after separation is an art and a skill. We can always learn more.

The following Developmental Parenting Guidelines will give you a general idea of this approach (even though no one would do or want to do all the things listed). You might want to keep in mind that although with this style the parent is a teacher and coach, parenting also means having fun, just being together, relaxing, and being a family. This style asks more of parents than the other styles, but the rewards can be greater.

GUIDELINES

THE "DEVELOPMENTAL" PARENTING STYLE

- Believes that the child is an individual, innately good, and deserving of respectful treatment no matter what their age. They do not call their child bad names, for example, "selfish," "stupid," or "lazy." They do not humiliate their child.
- Is warm, sensitive, caring, affectionate, responsive, loving, and protective. Is tuned in to the child's emotions.
- Is engaged with the child. Listens. Is interested in the child's world, communicates, teaches, coaches, cheers on, supports, and also makes sure there are fun and relaxing times, too.
- Understands that children are not miniature adults and that their brains, emotions, along with their bodies are still developing. They do not ask more of a child than the child can give or do.
- Believes in the child's ability to be successful in life. Helps the child learn social and emotional skills.
- Is not afraid of the child's disapproval and does not serve the child as does a permissive parent. Knows parenting is not a popularity contest.
- Encourages the child to identify and name feelings and helps them find acceptable ways of expressing them.
- Sets clear limits and rules and is consistent but not rigid. Gives reasons and explanations for limits. "Because I said so" is used carefully. The child knows what is expected.
- Has reasonably high expectations for effort and supports the child's efforts to succeed. Effort is more important than winning or achieving the highest grades.
- Helps the child appreciate his or her temperament and strengths and coaches them on life skills and habits so he or she can be happy, resilient, resourceful, and independent.
- Teaches children about options, good choices, and consequences.

  - Invites children to express their thoughts and preferences, even though the parent might make the final decision.

Do not ask more of a child than a child can give or do.

- Helps the child learn how to meet challenges, make good choices and weigh the consequences on self and others.
- Coaches children how to take responsibility for one's own actions and how to be accountable.

Uses Discipline to Teach and Build Skills

- *Focuses on behavior when correcting a child.* The child is not bad, but the behavior needs to change.
  - Points out how well the child did in the past.
  - Might ask for the child's help now on how to do better in the future.
  - Includes *a discussion about the better way to do something* when discipline is called for so the child learns to discriminate between options.

Check out *Appendix 7: When and When Not To Use the "I" Message*

- *Uses "Time-out" periods to help a child regain control of their emotions and behavior, and not as punishments.* Time-outs can be followed by a short discussion about making up the damage. Time-outs by themselves may not teach anything and children may not "think about what they did."
- *Is firm that there is cause and effect.* Misbehavior has a natural consequence and you have to "make it up" by taking responsibility for the behavior.

  - Example—a child drives her bike over the neighbor's flowers. She not only apologizes but then does something to fix the damage. Perhaps it might be working with the neighbor to replant and buying fresh plants from her allowance.

- *Allows greater and greater freedom and choices* as the child demonstrates responsibility.

A Few Examples of Developmental Parenting

Parents set limits. Within those limits children have choices. Two-year-old Amy is asked if she wants to be carried to bed or walk by herself. She doesn't choose the time she goes to bed or if she goes or not, but she learns that when she made a choice to be carried that her choice counted.

Parents choose discipline that teaches and provides solutions. Seventeen-year-old Billy has been cited for speeding in the family car. His discipline is to go to court with his parent and pay the ticket from his savings. He has to take a class on safe driving and he cannot use the car until he gets at least a B in that class and discusses what he learned with his parents. Billy learns that certain behaviors and attitudes have consequences but that he can also learn something positive from them.

Parents have expectations. Parents are clear about their expectations and these expectations are in line with what a child can actually do.

Developmental Parenting Has the Best Results down the Road

When parents take on this style of parenting, it will often take more thought and attention than other styles, but it can bring wonderful results for you and for your child. Just remember, don't worry if you mix it up with other styles of parenting. Just try your best to take the developmental approach when you can.

Monika and Roberto

Monika and Roberto are mostly developmental parents. They felt they were tuned into their children. Imagine how they felt learning that their Sam had a behavior problem at school, something they had not seen at home. By working together with the school, they helped him take responsibility for his behavior and how it affected others. Sam improved quickly.

Cody and Laura

In counseling with Megan's therapist, Cody came to recognize that he was more permissive and less involved than he thought. He took the developmental guidelines to heart and made a commitment to be a more engaged Dad. Laura admitted that she was often too rigid and that she needed to listen to the children better and become more flexible and supportive. These parents are fortunate that they have had the chance with a counselor to examine their parenting styles more closely. They knew they had to reduce the stress on the children. They found solutions from a mix of adjusting their parenting

Any Style of Parenting Can Be Too Extreme

It can be too hovering, too demanding, too smothering, too laid back, too developmental. Find your own combination that works for you and your child.

styles and how they, as parents, treated one another. They had to work together as a team. Privately, they have also been feeling guilty that they had let things get so far out of hand. But everyone is human, and it's important that they also remember that they have many strengths as people and as parents. They've made a lot of progress. They have overcome the worst of the negative intimacy. They can be calm, courteous, and diplomatic most of the time. They have more constructive ways to communicate, and they are now learning how to keep the children protected from the miserable middle. It's easier for them to focus on their parenting skills and styles. These are huge accomplishments and a testimony to their love for their children!

YOUR CHILD'S TEMPERAMENT AND MOVING

Divorce is like a big ship making its way through a sea of decisions and emotions. It leaves a wake. Try to make that wake as gentle as you can.

When parents separate and divorce, sometimes the family home must be sold or the family has to move out of a long-term rental. A change of residence is deeply unsettling to many children.

Here's an example of how children can be different within a family. Jill is 9 and always busy doing something and trying new things. She's out-going and seems to adjust to changes in routines and new places rather well. Her older sister, Lori, 13, however, likes things to move slower, more deliberately. She is rather shy and gets anxious with even little changes. She likes things to stay the same and accepts changes slowly. Michael is 8 and seems to handle change a bit better than Lori, but not as well as Jill. The children have lived in the family home for ten years. Now that it has to be sold, they must move to a new neighborhood. How can their parents help them?

Hopefully, these parents will do their best to find a home in the same school district unless the old school was unsatisfactory. Keeping the same school can be a big key to family adjustment. None of the children in this example would find a new school easy, particularly Lori.

When telling the children about an upcoming move, the parents can organize their new home search so the children can know they have things under control. The parents will give them a voice. They will let the children view some possible homes with them before the parents decide. They don't drag the children around to every possible home, but wait until they have narrowed their choices down to a few. The parents let the children have a say even though they don't make the final decision. Jill is action-oriented, so looking for a new place will help her cope. Her brother, eight-year-old Michael, might follow Jill's lead if Jill approves of the process and the new home. Lori on the other hand may refuse to go house shopping at first but will probably come along with the others.

PARENTING CHECKLIST

- ☐ Help your children feel secure in your love not just with words but also with action. Pay attention to them. Show them that they are loved and protected.

- ☐ Be a "warm" and sensitive parent. Listen well. Give hugs, pats, smiles, loving eye-contact, and encouragement. Use a kind tone of voice and endearments such as "honey," "sweetheart."

- ☐ Help your children learn about people and the world. Teach them social and emotional skills. Emphasize and value their strengths. Coach them on how to manage difficulties and interpret their experiences. Be a good example.

- ☐ Encourage academics and learning skills—attend school conferences, show interest, support. Help them enjoy learning. Monitor homework and grades.

- ☐ Get involved in their lives—attend activities, share projects, interests, and have fun together. Make sure they have time to just be kids.

- ☐ Use the "developmental" parenting style, especially with discipline. Fine tune your skills at including your older child in discussions and explanations.

- ☐ Monitor activities—know where your children are and with whom, including your teenagers.

- ☐ Be there for your child, either in-person or with texts, calls, tweets, and emails.

- ☐ Have similar House Rules and Safety Rules in both homes so children know what is expected of them. See that both you and the kids follow them.

- ☐ Give children chores and family responsibilities—appropriate to their ages and abilities. When families work together, they grow closer and stronger.

Be consistent and follow through. Don't give in just to keep the peace.

☐ Have high expectations—but not impossibly high. Realistic goals motivate. Appreciate effort as well as success.

☐ Be consistent and follow through. Have reasonable consequences. Don't give in just to keep the peace. When children make good choices and have a good attitude, give them more freedom.

☐ Keep kids out of the middle of your issues with the other parent. Protect them from seeing, hearing, or getting involved with your conflicts and negative intimacy. This is a priority.

☐ Be a good example. Show the children respect for the other parent by being calm, courteous, and diplomatic.

Childhood is a precious time for both parents and children. Play, laugh, have fun with, and enjoy your children. It all goes by too quickly.

NOTES FOR CHAPTER 10

1. There are many other ways to look at parenting styles (besides the four described here) and an Internet search of parenting styles will yield many perspectives. Your local adult education program might offer a class on parenting for today. You might meet other parents interested in boosting their effectiveness.

2. One style that has received a lot of attention is the "Gatekeeper" parent who believes that only he or she knows what is best for the child. In its extreme form, the Gatekeeper parent is threatened by the child's relationship with the other parent and actively attempts to keep the other parent powerless. This is often part of a cluster of destructive behaviors associated with "parent alienation."

3. Research shows that teens with parents who expect them to be accountable for their actions and who are warm and loving have far fewer problems with drinking. http://news.byu.edu/archive10-jun-parentingstyle.aspx Title: "Teen Drinking, High Accountability, High Warmth"

11

Put Together a
First-Rate Parenting Plan

A Useful and Solid Legal Plan
What Do You Have Now?
What Can Go into Parenting Plans
Other Things to Consider
Optional Private Agreements
The "Who Does What" List

A USEFUL AND SOLID LEGAL PLAN

A Parenting Plan (also called a Parenting Agreement) is usually a formal legal document that details your responsibilities and rights as parents and how you will share time with your child. A solid Plan provides you and the children with security, operating instructions, and predictability. It's not the only legal document about you and your children, but it is usually the most detailed and useful for the months and years ahead. Every state's requirement for family law documents can be different, and this book cannot offer you legal advice, but it can say that you and your child need your Plan to be first-rate—well-thought-out, easy-to-understand, useful, and crystal clear. You will refer to it often, especially when you and the other parent disagree.

You may already have a court order about parenting time and your rights as a parent to make decisions for your child. If you do, you can browse this chapter to see what you might want to add or delete the next time you update your arrangements. Also check out how to design your own private informal agreements to sort out the daily details. If you do not have a Plan, then this chapter can help you with resources and tips for constructing one. Be sure to consult with a family law attorney licensed in your state.

A Parenting Plan is probably the most important legal document you have about your children. It's also part of your "job description" as a coparent.

WHAT DO YOU HAVE NOW?

All parents who file for separation or divorce are required to identify in a legal document their choices about parenting time, custody, and access. This court form alone may not include a Parenting Plan. Typically, the Plan is a separate and optional document.

If you were never married and you want to coparent, it is still a good idea to make out a Parenting Plan. It's a very important document for you. First, however, you may want to establish legal "paternity." Check with your local court about requirements for the documents you need to file with the court to do this (see *Appendix 1: Never-Married CoParents*). Even if Dad is registered on the birth certificate as the father, in some venues this may not be enough to give him legal rights. Sad to say, within 3–5 years of parental separation, many Dads in these situations often fade away from their child's life. A Parenting Plan, no matter how short or simple, can help everyone stay connected.

Organize and Protect Your Legal Documents

What formal papers do you have? An official court form for custody only? A Parenting Plan, a Marital Settlement Agreement, or papers establishing paternity? Take stock. Then, if you are just starting out, go online to your local court's website and read about the legal documents you need. If you can, hire a family law attorney to work with you. Many counties or courts now have Legal Aid offices if you cannot afford an attorney.

Do you have a folder where you keep the paper copies of important legal papers? For example, do you have legal papers about your separation, custody, divorce, paternity, and your child's birth certificates? If you don't, think about putting that folder together now. If you don't have copies of these documents, it's a good idea to get them and put them in one place. Having PDF-format copies of your forms on your computer is also useful.

Custody? Know the Correct Legal Terms for You

Legal terms do matter! *Please remember* that the legal terms you choose for custody, access, and parenting time are extremely important, especially if you want to move out of the area with the children or are afraid the other parent might do this. If you are negotiating custody now, before you agree on terms, do some homework. Ask an attorney exactly how these terms are interpreted in your state and home court. Go online and read the actual statutes for your state on parenting time, custody, access, and visitation. Be sure to get detailed information on how "joint legal custody" works when it is just a general term or when it is spelled out.

WHAT CAN GO INTO PARENTING PLANS

Parenting Plans include the basic legal terms described above but also can go beyond these fundamentals to the next level of detail. For example, you can include the actual schedule for sharing time with your child and your agreements about how you will handle your children's education, transportation, medical and dental, activities, travel, and other items you may want to consider.[1]

Appendix 2: Parenting Plans, Online Resources, and Referrals has URLs for states and courts with downloadable model Plans you can look at and then modify to suit yourself. It's a good idea to see if your county or state has its own forms you can review or download. Search for *"family court+Parenting Plans+the name of your state or county"*. Not all states or courts have Parenting Plans or guidelines online. But you might want to check out the online forms and guidelines from Alaska, Arizona, and Orange County in California. These are especially helpful. Note that these schedules do not always agree and may not reflect the latest research on the best way to share parenting time for different ages of children, especially children under five years of age.

Here are a few things that may not be covered in the online Plans.

1. **A stated goal for your Plan**. Downloadable Plans may or may not have a space for you to write in these goals for your coparenting and for your child. You can use the goal you wrote in Chapter 3 and expand on it if you like. You might call it a preamble, mission statement, or the purpose of the Plan. You decide.
2. **Standards of Conduct**. It's helpful if you can include your own Standards of Conduct in your Plan or at least include them in your private agreements. You can find some suggested standards in *Mom's House, Dad's House* beginning on page 185.
3. **Non-disparagement.** Many Parenting Plans today will also have a clause that says neither parent will speak badly or disparage the other parent in any way to the child or where the child can observe or overhear the parent talking to someone else. Cody and Laura are more respectful and diplomatic now, but they put this clause in their Parenting Plan anyway.
4. **High conflict or low trust.** If you have a problem with conflict or trust, the rule of thumb is: (a) be sure that you put in a higher level

Once you have a legal Plan, follow it. Don't pick and choose what to follow. Do the right thing.

of detail in your Plan so there is no question about what something means and how it can be interpreted, (b) have proper "default" and "consequences" for times when a parent goes against the Plan as shown below, and (c) pay close attention to the warning below on the "Discuss and Divide" option. Laura insisted that these provisions also be in their Plan.

Question: How do we start with an actual Plan? We already disagree about where our kids will go to school.

Answer: Take it step by step. Look at the suggestions in Chapters 3, 4, and 5 on how to get along with the other parent. Consider using a family mediator. Many parents, even those who do get along fairly well, still use a family mediator to help them put the entire Plan together.

OTHER THINGS TO CONSIDER

Making decisions. Day-to-day decisions are nearly always made by the parent the child is with at the time, but what about choices of schools, activities, or serious medical treatment? Who does what about medical appointments, school projects, sports or lessons, and activities? Transportation? Costs? For each topic, be very specific in your Parenting Plan about how decisions will be made. Here are some options:

- **Discuss and Decide Together**—This option assumes you can reach an agreement without a lot of argument.

- **Dividing Final Say**—Discuss it together but one parent has the final say if you disagree.

- **Dividing Decisions**—Discussion is optional. One parent makes the decision for that activity or area. The other parent is kept up to date, but does not decide.

- **Call in a Mediator**. When you still can't agree, don't wait until the situation becomes more negative or disappointing. Before you get to a point of no return, use a mediator or a coparenting counselor with mediation experience.

Decide how you will you manage situations when a parent doesn't follow the Plan. Design some defaults or consequences. For example, if a parent is often more than 30 minutes late bringing their child to the other parent, maybe the "waiting" parent should have the option to keep the child 30 minutes longer than they were scheduled to have the child with them. This is just one suggestion. Only you can design a default or consequence that makes sense to you.

Where will the children live? Ideally your two homes will allow the children to go to school without a long commute and where going from one home to the other on transition day is not physically tiring, especially for the littlest ones. Trips longer than 20–25 minutes can be too stressful, especially in traffic. It's not always practical to have the two homes close together, but if you are going to coparent, it's a serious consideration.

If there is conflict and low trust, here's a reminder: Don't use the "Discuss and Decide Together" option. It can be like throwing gasoline on a fire. Consider dividing decisions instead—at least until things become more positive. For example, a Dad decides about music lessons, the Mom about gymnastics. If the days and times for these activities fall on the other parent's time, that parent has to agree to either bring the child or to allow the other parent to bring the child. If the activity requires a major time commitment, the parents should agree on how the child can attend practices and games or events.

Give some of your agreements a trial run. Before you sign your final legal Parenting Plan version, see how it works in real life. This trial run won't be practical for vacations or special days, but you could try things out during a week or two of a normal schedule.

Schedule revisions for your Plan, no less frequently than every year. The next chapter on schedules describes this in more detail.

Use a custody mediator or coparenting counselor or mediator if you and the other parent can't agree on something important in a reasonable amount of time. You can usually find a custody mediator either through your family court or one in private practice. Call your family court to find out if they have a free mediation service and if you are eligible for it. If the court does not have this service, you should still look for a private mediator to help you get yourself a good Plan.[2]

Finally, if you are doing this plan on your own, get a legal review. Ask a private attorney or an attorney at the Legal Aid office to look over your Parenting Plan and help you file your final Plan with the court. This is very important.

OPTIONAL PRIVATE AGREEMENTS

The devil is in the details

Private Agreements Are Detailed and Just between Parents

Decide if you want to put any of the items in the sections below into your legal Parenting Plan or in a Private Agreement. This is your choice.

Private Agreements go to the next level of detail. They spell out the day-to-day specifics that often don't belong in a formal legal Parenting Plan. But for some parents, writing things out in an informal agreement helps them focus and sort out some of the specifics. Example: in the formal Parenting Plan, Laura and Cody say that they will both actively support their children's schooling. But how? In their informal Private Agreement (which they did once they finished their Parenting Plan), they wrote down certain routines for homework they would both follow and how they would either share or divide the big school projects or volunteer efforts at school this year. Since this is their own private agreement, they can revise this anytime they want (without having to change their formal court-recorded Parenting Plan). Below are some things to consider for your own Private Agreement, or, if you wish, also for your Parenting Plan.

Transportation

Your Parenting Plan or court order might say who drives when it's time to transition from one home to the other, but not who drives in other situations such as when a teen offers your child a ride home or a parent's boyfriend or girlfriend picks up your child from school. You can put a statement in your Plan that says that only a parent can provide transportation, or anyone either parent designates. If you also make up your own Private Agreement, you can get down to more details and name the people who can drive your children and then later change that list easily by mutual agreement.

Days and Times

If your Plan is vague about when a child transitions from one parent to the other, for example "every other week from Thursday to Tuesday," is that clear enough for you? What is the actual time the child comes to the parent's home? If you don't have this detail, does it cause problems between you and the other parent? If it does, then the next time you revise your Plan you might want to add actual times of day so everyone knows what to expect. In the meantime, you can put together your own informal Private Agreement that includes these time details.

Who's in Charge?

Are you clear about when you become the responsible parent? For example, you take a child to school the day of the transition to the other parent. Is the time the child is in school your full responsibility or does the other parent take over as soon as you drop off your child at school? Example: If you child becomes ill shortly after school starts, who is responsible for going to the school, picking up your child, and taking care of him or her? Be specific.

Schooling and Homework: Your Academic Support

Your Parenting Plan should itemize your choice of schools or who and how you will make that decision. However, not many Plans go into details. For example, are you both clear who goes to teacher conferences, discusses progress with teachers and coaches, how you will handle detentions or suspensions, celebrate awards, support the homework projects that span the time between homes, and the daily homework? You might want to leave some of these details to Private Agreements or put them in a "Who Does What" list, discussed on the next few pages.

Elective Classes and Activities

Children may have lessons, a sport, or be in a club. They may have a part-time job or a regular get-together or parties with friends. How will you coordinate all these? Will you decide that you will each discuss and agree on every activity or just certain ones? And what happens if you can't agree? What happens if something like a sports team has practices that span the times the kids are with both of you? Will you both agree to see that the child attends all the practices and games? Earlier there was a recommendation that if there were serious disagreements or conflicts, parents would divide the authority and responsibility for different activities and electives. Whether you do that or not, you should come up with a way your child can make all their practices and games. Try to avoid situations where kids only have classes and practices on one parent's time because the other parent is against the activity.

YOUR IDEAS

Trips away From Home

Most Plans will have a provision saying a parent can't take a child out of state without the permission of the other parent, but what about trips in the state? Is any overnight okay with an itinerary to the other parent? What about trips of 50 miles or more with or without an overnight? Some parents want to know about such trips while others do not. You can describe what you want in your Plan or in a Private Agreement.

Last-Minute Changes, Emergency, Who's on Call

Have a plan about which parent will do what during these times. Which parent will be "on call" for that day? The resident parent? The parent working closest to the children? How will you contact each other about things like the homework or soccer cleats left behind, or that a child is ill and needs to be picked up from school? Pin this down before something happens and there's a mixup about who to contact.

House and Safety Rules

A Parenting Plan might have a sentence or two saying that you will each have your own House and Safety Rules and maybe that you will try to make these as much the same as possible. Your Private Agreement, however, can actually list these Rules or at least the ones that you will make the same in both homes. *Chapter 9: Find Ways to Help Your Child* discusses these in more detail. *Appendix 3: Safety Rules* and *Appendix 4: House Rules* have blank forms you can use to get you started.

THE "WHO DOES WHAT" LIST[3]

The mischief-maker in coparenting is "making assumptions." Because you once lived together, you assume you still know what the other parent will or should do. Once you are separated, it's wiser *not* to assume much of anything, especially the first year or two. It can waste your time, raise your blood pressure, and start arguments.

WHAT WOULD YOU DO?

Illness: Joey has the flu and he's living with Dad this week. He is in fifth grade and has already missed two important tests. Dad wants to contact the teacher but he doesn't have the contact information. He's irritated with Mom because he assumes she's in charge of getting the school information and has deliberately kept it from him. But Mom thinks that Dad, now that he has the children close to half of the time, has made his own contacts with the school and teachers and has all the emails and phone numbers that he needs. If this happened to you, what would you do to avoid this problem in the future?

Permission Slip: Claire is in ninth grade and needs a permission slip signed for an overnight school trip. The trip is today and this is the time she's with Mom. Sounds simple? But Claire got the slip when she was with Dad. The slip was supposed to be returned to school when she was with Dad but she lost it and didn't tell him. Mom solves it by going late to work, stopping by the school and signing the slip so Claire can leave that afternoon. If this happened in your family, what would be your solution?

Example of the Who Does What List

The Activity	Who Is Responsible?	Comments
The Family "Master Calendar." Who creates it and gives copies to the other parent?	Mom does January through June, Dad has it July through December.	Parents will use the online calendar.
Cheerleading schedule, uniforms, equipment and all costs	Dad is totally responsible for everything about this activity. Mom will support the team with the other Moms. Dad will give Mom copies of everything he gets about schedules and league business.	This includes all transportation, uniforms, singups, and other costs.
Debate team schedule, and all costs	Mom is totally responsible for everything about this activity. She will give Dad copies of everything she gets about schedules and events.	This includes all transportation costs and signups.
School-year calendar	Mom will get the school-year calendar and make sure Dad has a copy.	
Report cards	Each of us will ask the school for a separate report card. The report card will be signed by one of us after we discuss the report.	
School or activity permission slips	Mom will be responsible for seeing that either she or Dad signs the slips on time.	

The Who Does What List

The Activity	Who Is Responsible? Mom? Dad? Shared?	Comments?
The Family "Master Calendar"		
Church calendar		
School-year calendar, teacher and school contact information		
Sport or Activity: costs, decisions, calendar, paperwork		
Sport or Activity: costs, decisions, calendar, paperwork		
Sport or Activity: costs, decisions, calendar, paperwork		
Report cards		
School or activity permission slips		
Contact information for teachers, coaches, all adults in charge of any activity (Karate, baseball, ballet, Scouts, etc.)		
School projects that span the time in both homes		
Teacher conferences, detentions, and awards		
Daily and weekly homework assignments		
Results of MD, DDS visits, laboratory tests		
Medications: recent medications, allergies, names and dosages of current medications		
Health: making and keeping medical, dental, other medical-type appointments; restrictions, issues		
Updating the names, numbers of child's doctors and dentists, counselors, other health professionals		
Tutoring: schedule, payments, discussions about progress and goals		
Contact information for neighbors and the parents of the children's friends		
Teenager's transportation: license, gas, repairs, insurance, bus passes, bikes		
Clothing: purchase, repair		
Electronics: purchase, maintenance, software, apps		
Allowances, a teenager's job		

IMPORTANT

Once you decide on who does what, remember that no matter who has the responsibility for something, both of you should feel free to attend teacher conferences, Open House, special school events like presentations, recitals, concerts, games (but not necessarily practices), even if they fall on the other parent's time.

NOTES FOR CHAPTER 11

1. In *Mom's House, Dad's House*, Part III, you will find a list of Parenting Plan topics, a sample Plan, and sample negotiations. There are more than 80 pages in Part III devoted to the legal business, parenting plans, custody decisions, negotiations, and mediation.

2. In *Mom's House, Dad's House*, Chapter 15 is dedicated to selecting a mediator and how to use mediation wisely.

3. Pages 356–358 in *Mom's House, Dad's House* discusses day-to-day responsibilities in more detail.

12

Design a Winning and Workable Family Schedule

A Winning and Workable Parenting Schedule
Your Child's Temperament
Sharing Time with Your Child
Designing Your Schedule
How Some Parents Share Time
When More Overnights Are Not the Answer
More Secrets to Successful Scheduling

A WINNING AND WORKABLE PARENTING SCHEDULE

When you and the other parent were together, you may not have planned your calendar ahead for 12 months, 18 months, or longer, but once you no longer live together, this planning is necessary. Having to divide your children's time with their other parent may not be what you want, but here you are.

The basic message of this chapter is just common sense. The best schedule for being with Mom and Dad is not just what the children can *tolerate*, it's one that allows them to develop in a healthy way so they have their best chance with life. The way to success is to design a schedule that gives your children time and frequent communications with both of you. It gives them a routine that works for their age, needs, and personality, is flexible when it needs to be and is not tiring. It is one that's easy enough to understand and follow. A doable schedule is a big achievement!

Children in two homes can do very well with a schedule that meets their needs. But if the schedule asks too much of them or they don't see as much of a beloved parent as they need, they may not do well at all. It's a little like plants that grow strong and beautiful in full sun but don't do well in partial shade. The message here is that parents want to design a schedule that will allow their child to thrive.

Children are resilient but everyone has a breaking point. Don't press your luck.

YOUR CHILD'S TEMPERAMENT

How Much Change Is Just Enough?

. . . .

Children are the original work in progress.

They are not miniature adults—even the oldest teenagers. They are a different kind of thinking machine and they have their own timetable for how they will develop.

. . . .

Your Child's "T.L.C." The big question is how much change your child can handle and still develop normally. Parents want the best for their child, but there is no one-size-fits-all solution because each child is different. Children come hardwired with their own temperament and then their life experiences shape them even further. *Mom's House, Dad's House* explains it in this way:

> "The ability of your child to withstand change is often a combination of many things you *can* control, including your support, your love, and your care. But a child's basic makeup needs to be considered. Think of your child's uniqueness as TLC.
>
> > T = Temperament and resilience
> > L = Level of development and prior experience
> > C = Constitution and physical sturdiness."[1]

Parents may describe their children's temperaments as active, quiet, shy, easygoing, determined, sensitive, resilient, high-strung. Now add a child's physical, emotional, and intellectual development. Perhaps they have been sheltered from harsh experiences or have actually been through quite a bit with their family. Then, there's their "constitution," an old-fashioned word that means a person's general health and strength. Some children are sturdy and never seem to get sick, while others tire easily, and still others are frail. You know your child. You are the expert on this subject. Put this all together and you have your child's TLC.

As you think about your own child's TLC, measure how well you think they have handled change or frightening experiences. It's helpful to remember that helping a child adjust to separation and divorce means taking into account a child's TLC, experiences, their relationship with their parents, what frightens them, and what parents do to help them cope and feel secure. For example, a sensitive, shy child with a fragile TLC may not do well with change at certain stages of life. But if this child has a strong trusting bond with a nurturing and sensitive parent, he or she may be able to manage big changes, especially when they are done carefully and the parents are not in conflict and can work together.

SHARING TIME WITH YOUR CHILD

Time with Each Parent

Usually, both children and parents want to see as much of each other as possible, but divorce means that children no longer see their parents together except on specific occasions like an Open House, a birthday, or an afterschool activity. Sadly, in some families children never see their parents together at all. For the parents, their separation means they no longer have the freedom to be with their child at any time they want. Instead, their time together is decided by court orders and Parenting Plans until they can agree and develop a more flexible coparenting style and make up their own schedule.

Your coparent will be an important person in your child's life forever. As long as there is no risk to your child or to you, be sure your schedule allows your child to have a meaningful life with both of you.

> **The biggest adjustment your children make is being with only one of you at a time.**
>
> They have to cope with their longing for the parent who is not there, less time with each of you, and rarely having both parents together in one place at the same time.

The Many Dimensions of Time

Coparenting is not all about equal time.[2] It's about giving your child two active and involved parents, and giving you, the parent, the opportunity to raise your child. So, when you plan your schedule, keep in mind that a child sleeping in the same house with a parent is a very important part of parenting, but it is not the only way to be an active parent or keep your bond strong. Here are some examples of different ways to share time with your child:

- **Time together with your child in the same place**
  - *Overnights:* the bedtime rituals, the routines, waking up in the same house together.
  - *Separately:* maybe you are doing laundry or working in the yard while your child is playing with a friend or doing homework in another part of the house.
  - *Together:* meals, feeding, baths, dressing, playing, doing projects, chores, riding in the car, coaching, playing games, talking, hobbies, watching TV, activities, church.

- **Separated from your child but your child is still your responsibility**

Quality can't substitute for actual time, and actual time cannot make up for poor quality. Everyone needs both.

- * Your child is in school, child care, camp, at a lesson, practice, job, out with friends.

- * You are at work, running errands, socializing, and involved in doing things that support your child as well as your adult life.

- * You are doing something for your child—setting up appointments, working on a school committee, church group, buying uniforms, books, getting resources, and so forth.

- **Separated from your child but in contact**

  - * You are texting, phoning, emailing, tweeting, sending videos, photos, and using other electronic and traditional ways to stay connected.

Aim for less stress all around.

DESIGNING YOUR SCHEDULE

As you design your schedule, keep these different considerations and your children's needs in mind.

Babies and Toddlers Have Special Needs

If you have a child younger than four or five, especially if you have a baby or a toddler, realize that some of the latest research suggests that children of these ages and stages of development may not do well over time with changes in caregivers, routines, or places where they sleep.[3] Please remember that young children and babies need more than food and other essentials, to do well. They need a consistent daily routine that meets their needs and loving warmth and care from their parents and caregivers. The youngest ones do not yet understand abstract concepts like time, so for many of them being transported to another house for a night 3 or 4 times a month can be like 3 or 4 "first times" in a new place even when it is with people who love them dearly. Parents should seriously consider the different dimensions of time listed above and find ways where their little ones can have a stable routine with both parents without changing where they sleep. As the child grows older, a gradual increase in full days and overnights at their other home can happen naturally.

Ages Five and Older

- Try not to ask your child of any age to make too many changes over a short period of time.[4] It's exhausting and confusing. Children don't learn well when they are tired.

- Use your child's TLC as a guide, not just his or her age. No matter how intelligent a child may be, living in two homes is still a demanding emotional and physical experience. Children are resilient but also incredibly vulnerable.

- Your coparent will be an important person in your child's life forever. As long as there is no risk to your child or to you, be sure your schedule allows time for your child and the other parent to be together.

- Children want a relationship—not just time—with both parents. Will the schedule you design give that to your child?

- Play close attention to what frightens your child and how well your child seems to bounce back after disappointment or something scary. For some children, changes, even good ones, might be frightening.

- If your child has had some serious upsetting experiences such as the loss of a pet, a grandparent, or a treasured friend has moved away, be especially understanding. Sometimes these changes can help a child see that life goes on okay. Other children, however, become even more sensitized to possible future losses.

- If you have a child who is frail or exceptionally sensitive, try to keep the routine as even-keeled and low-stress as possible. Going back and forth may not work, and you may need to postpone overnights in two homes until the child matures and their health improves.

"I can often tell which children are having a hard time with the schedule. They are tired, even exhausted. It is difficult for them to learn."
—A school nurse

Your Schedule: School Year, Summer, Holidays, Vacations

This is your child. You want your child to have the best possible schedule that is healthy for them and rebuilds their sense of basic trust in life and in their parents. If it turns out that overnights are not a good idea for your child now, then use the many other ways to share time to keep your bond strong until your child can manage overnights easily.

If you are designing your first schedule, go to *Appendix 2: Parenting Plans, Online Resources, and Referrals*, and look at some of the websites from different states listed there. Some have sample calendars available. Most calendars use a repeating pattern for the school year for parenting time whether it is rotating a week with each parent or a routine of more time at one parent's house than at the other's. Summer vacations, holidays, and special days may be more flexible, but usually there needs to be firm schedules for vacations, child care, summer camps, or summer school.

We can pretend to care, but we can't pretend to be there.

Long-Distance Parenting

Parents can coparent across many miles, even across states or countries. This is a special kind of parenting, one that is easier today with Skype, email, videos, texts, and Twitter. However necessary this arrangement might be, being separated like this means far fewer hugs, outings, and just hanging out together. A child knows that the parent is not easily available or right around the corner. Their parent can't be on the sidelines or in the audience or at an Open House. Still, with consistent, thoughtful effort, you can develop your own brand of active parenting.[5] Don't give up. Be creative.

Some Big Questions About Your Schedule

The schedule you come up with has to jump over a few hurdles. Do the days you pick help your child settle down and feel safe? Are middle-of-the-school-week transitions easy and low-stress or complicated or tiring? Does the schedule help your child feel like they can cope with this new way of living?

Even for school-age children, shifting homes every two or three days may be too much for them. For other children, it works well because they feel best when they see each parent nearly every day and the days with one parent or the other are always the same. Still, for other children, staying in one place with one parent for the school week with generous time on weekends with the other parent works best. The schedule should be what helps your child to thrive. It should not be a numbers game where overnights are determined by money and support considerations. As parents, we usually want as much time as possible with our children. But children need both parents. We have to share.

• •

"Transition" or "exchange" are words some coparents use to describe the process when children shift homes and parents. Children usually just say, "I'm with my Mom" or "I'm going to be with my Dad."

• •

Going Back and Forth

If you are new at coparenting after separation, here are some tips. For your child, going back and forth between homes, living there for a set number of days, or just staying overnight can be like going on a trip. If you have read the *Mom's House, Dad's House* books, you already know that children want to feel like they belong in each home and have that sense of "my own things, here." Successful coparents report that their children have their own space and beds at each home. They have all or most of what their children need at each home so there are no big bags or suitcases to lug back and forth. That's fine. But, there's still the process of making that transition from one home to the other. Here's one way to organize the shift for yourself and the kids.

- Get ready
- Know the destination
- The "transition" or "exchange" of the children
- The "re-entry" of children into the other home. How they settle in and how their parents adjust.

Get ready. This is that stretch of time where parents and kids collect things to go with them to the other parent. There may be a bag, a backpack, electronics, sports equipment, musical instruments, favorite games, books, electronics, and clothes. Unless it's a weekend, there is usually homework and school things. At the same time, the parent is figuring out how to get everything and everyone there on time.

Know the destination. This sounds simple, but the "transition" may happen at different places and even at different times, so it's helpful for everyone to be clear every time. The destination may be to school or an activity where, once it is over, the child goes home with the other parent. Or it's a trip to the other parent's home where the children, with their gear, will transfer their lives to the other parent for a while.

The transition. Once the parent and the kids reach their destination, there is the exchange where the kids "transition" from one parent to the other. There are many examples and options that can help you figure out a way to make this as low stress and as positive as possible. Check out the page numbers at the end of this chapter for more information in *Mom's House, Dad's House* and *Mom's House, Dad's House for KIDS*.[6]

Re-entry. Goodbye and Hello. This phase is the period of time it takes a child and a parent to settle in and re-start their lives together. For kids, it's a kind of "climate" change. It can begin when the the kids arrive at the other home or as soon as they pile in the car with the "receiving" parent. This "re-entry" is a very important time for children. Each child has their own way of managing the re-entry. It's worth learning more about it.[7] Let's not forget that you and the "receiving" parent have to get reoriented too. It can be a gut wrench to have to watch your children leave you, even when you know it's the best thing for them to have a relationship with the other parent. On the receiving end, there can be a sense of joy and relief, but also you resume your routine of having the children live with

A child has to learn how to say goodbye to one parent while also saying hello to the other. "It's weird, it's confusing," said one 10-year-old girl.

you once again. And then kids are kids—don't be surprised if someone has forgotten something.

HOW SOME PARENTS SHARE TIME

If you have explored the different time arrangements explained in *Mom's House, Dad's House*, pages 172–178, and the examples described on the websites suggested in *Appendix 2: Parenting Plans, Online Resources, and Referrals* in this book, you already know the common timesharing schedules and how different they can be from each other. Here, however, are some schedules you may not find explained often. These are some other ways parents can be flexible in order to put their children's needs first.

Cari is 6, Raoul 9, and Rosa 10.

Their parents have been separated for five years. The first four years, Cari lived with her mother and spent certain daytimes with her father on weekend days. But Raoul and Rosa, then 5 and 6, would stay some weekend nights with him. First it was just Friday nights, then, as they grew older, Friday and Saturday. Then it increased to Thursday night through Sunday. Cari usually stayed only one night. When the parents thought that the children could manage a longer period of time away from Mom, they changed their schedule to a week with Mom and a week with Dad with 1, sometimes 2 dinners a week with the other parent on their off week. Unfortunately, while the older children are doing well with the arrangement, Cari is not and she still seems to need longer times with Mom. The parents have decided to keep the new schedule for the older two children but have Cari on the old schedule. This trial period can help everyone.

Aaron is 13 and Paula is 14.

The children have been in a rotating two-week schedule between their homes for six years and it has worked well. Now, however, both children want to change the schedule. Paula wants to live primarily with her Mom and Aaron with his Dad. A child's desire to be more with one parent in their teen years is common. The downside is that the siblings will be separated from each other for the first time in their lives, and the parents will not have both children at the same

Reminder

If the exchanges or transitions happen at school or daycare, it seems to be easier for many families. If the parents have issues that flare up with face-to-face contact, avoid that contact and the children don't have to worry if there will be an argument or dirty looks.

time except on some weekends. The current compromise has been to try a rotation of three weeks where two weeks are with the parent they want, then one week when Aaron and Paula are together with one parent. For example, Aaron would be with Dad and Paula with Mom for two straight weeks. This would include a midweek dinner and perhaps some activities with the other parent. The third week, the two teens would be together with either Mom or Dad. Then the schedule would start all over again. The problem was that it looked good on paper, but it didn't feel good to anyone. So, after a trial period of two months, they all decided to try two straight weeks with the parent they wanted, then two weeks together with Mom, then two weeks together with Dad, then back to the parent they wanted. Time will tell if this arrangement works out well or not.

Don't agree to do things you can't manage just to look good or compete with the other parent. That's not what coparenting is about.
—A coparent Dad

WHEN MORE OVERNIGHTS ARE NOT THE ANSWER

Being a family means living together and overnights are a key part of it. But sometimes more overnights with a parent can make things worse. Here are some examples where a parent's desire to have more overnights needed to be put on hold because the child's needs took priority.

Allie is 8 months old.

Her parents separated three months ago. Her father was away on business most of the time after she was born, so he has not taken over any day-to-day care for her. Allie has a Nanny who has been with her since birth from 11 to 7 each day while Mom works outside the home. Since Dad wants to be an active father, he realizes that if Allie is to bond with him he must change his work schedule so he can commit to seeing her regularly. Both parents understand that Allie is closely bonded with her mother as well as the Nanny. They agree she needs a consistent environment and schedule, so they decide there will be no overnights away from her mother until she is much older.

    The parents created a schedule where for the first month Dad saw Allie 4–5 times a week between 5 p.m. and 6 p.m. at Mom's house with the Nanny there to coach him and provide Allie with a sense of continuity. During this time, Allie became more and more comfortable with Dad. She eventually allowed him to feed and change her without a fuss. The second month, the Nanny busied herself with other tasks while Dad took over all of Allie's needs and often stayed longer. Allie looked forward to seeing her father, and as she grew older Dad would take her out in her stroller on weekends and to visit his parents for several hours. So far Allie has her mother every morning and at night if she awakes. She has her Nanny in the afternoon, and her father for a few hours for usually 3 to 4 evenings during the week. It's a balance that works for her. Her parents' work schedules may change and then the schedule will have to adjust, but the frequent contact Allie has with her father now is giving them both the opportunity to form that very important bond. Nonetheless, Mom has to deal with her discomfort at having Dad in her home, and Dad has to manage his desire to have Allie in his own environment instead of in Mom's home. But for now, it's the best they can do in order for infant Allie do well. With Dad's consistent visits with Allie, there will be a time when he and Allie can be in his home more including overnights. When will that time come? No one can say for sure, but it should be when Allie can manage it.

Danny, 6, doesn't do well with change.

He is a sensitive, shy child with few friends. He is easily frightened. He is very attached to his mother who has been home with him all his life but he eagerly looks forward to seeing his father when he returns home usually after dinner. When the parents decided to separate and divorce, they knew Danny would be faced with many major changes. They wisely decided to take things slowly and change one thing at a time. Mom would remain in the house and not go back to work right away so Danny could adjust to the big change of not seeing his father every night. Then they would cooperate on ways Dad and Danny could be together, at first without overnights. Dad would make work arrangements so he could pick up Danny after school two or three times a week, have an early dinner with him and then back to Mom for bath and bedtime. On either Saturday or Sunday, Danny and Dad would be together most of the day at Dad's new place working on model airplane projects. Dad could teach him how to use the computer for games and Skype so they could see each other via computer. As Danny becomes more comfortable with Dad's new home and the fact that his parents are apart, he can then begin to spend overnights with Dad.

The next round of changes Danny will face will be far less time with his mother when she returns to work and he starts afterschool care. Danny needs more, not less attention from his parents now. The key for Danny is not the time each parent deserves, but what time schedule will help him stay healthy and develop normally.

Emma is 14 and lives with her father.

Physically, Emma, who is mature for her age, never seems to get tired or sick. Her attitude is negative and bossy. She brags to her friends that her Dad is easy to manipulate and that she can do whatever she wants. Secretly, she feels no one cares enough about her to set limits or support her interests in nature and animals. She has been skipping school, and Dad suspects she is smoking pot and is sexually active. He worries that Emma will run away. Emma's mother had moved 70 miles away two years ago but Emma refused to visit her. Dad and Mom did not insist. Mom, now concerned about Emma, has moved back to town and wants Emma to live with her half-time. Emma refused to stay even one overnight. Mom and Dad have a lot of work to do if they are going to reduce the real risks ahead for Emma. Emma has many urgent needs, and the parents insisting on "overnights" is not the answer. The parents need to immediately answer Emma's cry for help to reverse her downward spiral.

Dad and/or Mom would be advised to start family counseling immediately with someone who specializes in teens. They can do this even if Emma refuses to cooperate at first. A big first step is showing Emma that her parents are trying to work together and that she can't play one of them against the other. Mom and Dad can learn something about setting up reasonable boundaries, House Rules, and consequences, while also insisting on a medical checkup, and drug testing. They can show Emma they are truly interested in her needs and interests even if she doesn't live with Mom right away. Mom can find ways to become closer with Emma without the overnights. Besides inviting Emma to go shopping and decorating her room in Mom's new apartment, Mom can drive Emma to and from school and activities, volunteer at school, and both parents can be more present at events, tutoring, and other things the counselor might suggest.

Freddy is 3 and lives most of the time with his mother.

He spends two days and nights a week with his father. His parents separated four months ago and have been in open conflict about their differences. Freddy was not sleeping well before the separation but now he wakes up crying several times a night. He has gone back to sucking his thumb and needing a diaper. He is clingy and unhappy. He cries hysterically when Mom leaves him with Dad, but then when Dad brings him back to Mom he has a tantrum. Both parents are worried about Freddy. But Dad thinks that if he doesn't have Freddy with him for at least two overnights a week that Freddy will gradually pull away from him. Mom wants Freddy and his Dad to have a close relationship, but she wants to stop the overnights for now. Freddy needs something to change for the better and as soon as possible. Obviously, Mom and Dad must save their conflict for times when Freddy can't see or hear them, but correcting this is just the first step in helping Freddy. He needs a thorough medical checkup to identify any physical issues that are adding to his obvious distress. Because Freddy is so distraught and the parents are at odds, a child expert that the pediatrician recommends may be able to help them shape a routine that allows Freddy to get back on track and also allows Dad and Freddy to keep that strong bond.

Bottom Line: A Schedule That Looks Logical on Paper May Not Work in Real Life

Each child has his or her own pace of development for processing information, new experiences, emotions, and handling their growing bodies. A schedule that looks okay on paper may not work for their development in life. Before you finalize a schedule, read all of this book, especially *Chapter 9: Find Ways to Help Your Child* and *Chapter 10: Fine Tune Your Parenting Style*. Please be prepared to watch for your child's unhealthy reactions to any changes.

MORE SECRETS TO SUCCESSFUL SCHEDULING

Children need to feel they have a say.

Ask the Kids

- Before you finalize a schedule, ask your older children what they think. You don't need to change your Plan, but you do need to ask.
- Then, once you've tried this schedule for a few weeks, ask all your children again how the schedule is working for them. Again, you don't need to do what they want, but you do need to ask.
- Immediately make changes to the schedule and activities if a child shows signs of stress.
- Ask your children what things they enjoy doing with you the most. What do they want more or less of? Give them a chance to give their opinion.

The schedule is not a numbers game where overnights are determined by money and support considerations. It's should be about what works best for your child.

Monika and Roberto had a casual conversation with Sam about how the schedule was for him. He seemed surprised that they asked and just said it was "Okay" but that sometimes he wanted to stay longer with Dad. So, Monika and Roberto told him that they would try and make that happen.

Be Clear about the Details

Schedules only work well when everyone is crystal clear about what's supposed to happen—where, the time you arrive and leave, what to bring, who drives. If you don't have these details pinned down, things can get scrambled.

Use a Calendar the Kids Can See

A calendar is a symbol of order, stability, and predictability. It's an easy way to get a lot of things done at once. Keeping a calendar up to date, especially if you have more than one child, is a challenge, even with today's electronic aids. Some parents use online calendars that they update from their smart phones, computers, or electronic tablets such as iPads. Other parents keep a paper-and-pencil calendar where everyone can see it. It is often a big write-on calendar with lots of room for new items. Some kids keep their own reminders in notes in their pockets or in their own smart phones.

Review and revise your Plan and private agreements no less frequently than once a year

Okay! Let's say you now have a schedule and it seems to be working well. Congratulations. This is a huge win for everyone. But time will pass, and the schedule needs to keep up with everyone. Your children will grow and their needs will change (and perhaps yours as well). A schedule that works for this year may not be good for you or your child next year.

Set a date with your coparent to review your Plan, Schedules, and Private Agreements every year. Some people plan to do it on the same day or week every year, such as the first week in February so they can plan for the coming school year and summer camps. That's also a good time to consider the plusses and minuses of increasing or decreasing time together with your child.

Follow your agreements, court orders, and Parenting Plan. This can't be said enough. It's that important.

Follow Your Agreements, Court Orders, and Parenting Plans

The rules are strict. Just as child and spousal support must be paid, agreements about your rights and responsibilities must be followed, until you and the other parent both agree to make changes. Once a parent bends an agreement to suit his or her purposes without first getting an okay from the other parent, coparenting begins to sink. Be a team player.

Try to do what you agreed to do or were ordered to do by the court. If you don't follow the agreements, conflict (and eventually costly court action) is probably in your future. If you need changes and the other parent won't negotiate, then consider using a mediator, or as a last resort call a lawyer.

Once you have put together a solid Parenting Plan and a calendar, you can breathe a sigh of relief. You now have coparenting roadmaps. It takes heartfelt thought and effort to put together arrangements that both parents and the children can live with. High fives all around. This is a major accomplishment. You will probably refer to both of them for day-to-day living and resolving disagreements. While parts of your Plan and your calendar should change as your needs change, your basic Plan, along with your goals as coparents, can still be your guides for the road ahead.

Once a parent bends an agreement to suit his or her purposes without first getting an okay from the other parent, coparenting begins to sink. Be a team player.

NOTES FOR CHAPTER 12

1. Go to pp. 135–136 in *Mom's House, Dad's House* to read more about TLC. They describe children's temperaments, development, and experiences, and how important it is to pay attention to these differences when designing a schedule.

2. Pages 158–170 in *Mom's House, Dad's House* describes five dimensions of sharing parenting time: 1) Overnight, 2) Together time, 3) Outside activity time, 4) Holidays, special days, entertainment, and recreation, 5) Time away from both parents. In this Toolkit, these dimensions are arranged somewhat differently and expanded. You can choose which approach makes the most sense for you. The objective is the same, and that is to look at time with your child as having many different ways of being together.

3. *Mom's House, Dad's House*, pp. 168–178, has descriptions of schedules in detail.

4. Appendix 2 at the back of the book, "Some Other Resources," provides a link to a paper that summarizes important research on the risks and benefits of shared parenting including attention to research studies regarding the youngest children (under SOME OTHER RESOURCES).

5. In *Mom's House, Dad's House*, Chapter 18, pp. 280–297, the entire chapter is devoted to long-distance parenting.

6. *Mom's House, Dad's House for KIDS*, pp. 52–75, covers many topics for children, such as one home or two, re-entry, going back and forth, holidays, and issues kids have about the schedule.

7. *Mom's House, Dad's House*, pp. 72–73, discusses re-entry, in "Know Your Style of Settling In."

Epilogue

. . . .

Two and a Half Years Later

Monika and Roberto

Monika and Roberto work together as a team and are grateful for the way they support one another and their children. They meet all the Basic CoParenting Guidelines and are flexible whenever possible. Sam began living half-time with his Dad when he turned 9 and seems to manage the two homes well. When he asks to spend more time with either parent, the parents usually agree. Nell is still primarily living with her mother and stepdad and is a happy, sunny child but she does miss her brother. These parents protect the relaxed, flexible way they communicate and resolve differences. They are mindful of each other's privacy and routinely do email and text updates as well as doing a few things as a combined family. Monika married her boyfriend, Vern. They are talking about adding to the family. Roberto still doesn't like the idea that another man has so much time with his children, but he now trusts Vern and appreciates that Vern supports their coparenting arrangement. Roberto himself is newly engaged to a woman with a child a bit younger than Nell. These parents have moved on, but honor their past and their coparenting with their mutual respect and consideration. They have a healthy relationship and it is allowing their children to thrive. Everyone benefits!

Cody and Laura

Cody and Laura meet all the Basic CoParenting Guidelines now thanks to the way they used the Limited CoParenting Guidelines and to what they learned in counseling for Megan's eating disorder. There, they learned more about parenting and what Megan and their other children truly needed. Laura now appreciates that Cody does deeply love his children and Cody appreciates Laura's protectiveness and dedication to them. The biggest changes are that even though they still have some negative emotions and expectations about one another, these emotions are not dictating their decisions or reactions. The children have experienced their parents' teamwork and the family's overall stress level is now reasonable. The children are grateful their parents have stopped their arguing and sniping. When Cody and his girlfriend parted, he moved into his own apartment. Seven-year-old Matt now spends about one-third of his time with his father.

The twin girls wanted to have one home base with their mother, and Cody agreed as long as they stay with him on long weekends twice a month. He has become heavily involved in the girls' soccer team and is now an assistant coach. The girls often stay longer with their Dad if the time is connected with one of their practices or games. Megan appears to be doing well with her eating issues, but the parents have been advised that she could relapse easily. Alicia, however, is not doing as well in school, and the parents are in discussion with teachers about next steps. Without a working coparenting relationship, Cody and Laura and their children would not enjoy the less stressful and more enjoyable family life they have now nor would they be as good partners for solving their children's problems. Cody has recently become engaged to a woman with two teenagers. Laura started dating about seven months ago, much to her daughters' surprise and intense curiosity.

Remember That Your CoParent Loves the Children as Much as You Do

Along with the joys and satisfactions of raising children there are also many surprises and crises. If you can successfully coparent, you can take comfort that you have a partner in parenting who is just as invested in your children's health and well-being as you are, and who can also, at least potentially, support you as a parent. You and the other parent may never be close friends, but you are not parenting alone and your children can have both of you on their journey.

Mastering the CoParent Highway

Becoming a coparent is a life-changing experience. You no longer parent together under one roof and to your credit you have taken on this new coparenting way to raise your children. At times, it can feel like you are learning how to parent all over again. Fortunately, now you have many tools to choose from to help you map your journey on the CoParenting Highway. Be patient with yourself and with the other parent, too. It takes time and effort to boost and adjust your parenting, master effective, businesslike ways to communicate with one another, solve problems, manage negative intimacy, keep your child's needs up front, follow the Basic Guidelines, and on top of all that become calm, courteous, and diplomatic—at least most of the time. It's a lot!

The prize is a healthy family life and children who thrive. That is worth all your efforts many times over.

Appendix 1

Never-Married CoParents

• • • • • • • • • • • • • • • • • •

State laws may be different so it's important that parents check out the requirements for establishing paternity by consulting with a lawyer in their state. In some places, the father and mother may only need to sign an affidavit soon after the birth of their child to establish the father's legal paternity. Ask these questions:

1. Is the father's name on the birth certificate enough?
2. Does the father also have to file a court form to register himself formally as the father?
3. Does filing this court form establish a legal basis for requests for parenting time and other parenting rights?
4. Does filing this court form also establish the father's responsibility for child support?

Appendix 2

Parenting Plans, Online Resources, and Referrals

• • • • • • • • • • • • • • • • • •

Mom's House, Dad's House, pages 183–251, describes the elements of a Parenting Plan in detail, has a sample plan, describes how to negotiate a Plan on your own, and explains how to use a mediator to act as an unbiased third person who can help you come to a solution and agreement.

State Courts: Parenting Plans, Court Forms, and Time Share Schedules for Children of Different Ages

- Links to All States *http://family.findlaw.com/child-custody/custody-forms/state-child-custody-forms%281%29.html*
- Arizona Family Courts, Model Parenting Time Plans for Parent/Child *www.azlawhelp.org/documents/ModelParentingTimeGuide.pdf*
- California Family Courts, Orange County, Parenting Plan Guidelines *www.occourts.org/media/pdf/parenting-plan-guidelines.pdf*
- Alaska Family Courts *www.courts.alaska.gov/shcplan.htm*

SOME ONLINE CALENDARS FOR FAMILIES

Be sure to read the terms and conditions for each website before signing on.

www.cofamilies.com

A free online calendar that you, the other parent, and the children can develop, modify, and access anytime. Includes automatic notifications, and a complete history of schedules and communications—all sharable with your partner, caregivers, and children. Includes notes and messages to one another.

www.OurFamilyWizard.com

A subscription service for your private and shared family calendars, that includes a message board, reminders, online access to documents, and a resource section.

SOME OTHER COPARENT WEBSITES

www.coparentingtoday.com

A coparenting blog, free articles, and ways to buy Isolina Ricci's books, *The CoParenting Toolkit; Mom's House, Dad's House: Making Two Homes for Your Child;* and *Mom's House, Dad's House for KIDS: Feeling at Home in One Home or Two.*

www.UpToParents.org

For separated, divorcing, and divorced parents, with resources, articles, information, and referrals for family mediation, and a newsletter.

www.ProudToParent.org

Specifically for parents who were not married to each other, with short articles, videos, and mediation resources.

SOME OTHER RESOURCES

For research on sharing custody and parenting times, the summary report *"Custody & Parenting Time: Summary of current information and research"* is from a subcommittee of the Family Law Advisory Committee for the State of Oregon. It summarizes a review of the research and offers recommendations. Key research on parenting time schedules and factors for risky and successful coparenting and child adjustment are listed at the end of this report. The 13-page summary can be found at http:// courts.oregon.gov/OJD/docs/OSCA/cpsd/courtimprovement/familylaw/ CustodyPTR.pdf.

REFERRALS

Referrals to coparenting counselors, family mediators, and family law professionals. For referrals in your area, check the online sites of the National Counseling Association, American Association of Marriage and Family Therapists, the American Psychological Association, the Family Law Section of the American Bar Association, or your State Bar Association, the Collaborative Law associations, and your state's listings of Licensed Clinical Social Workers and Marriage and Family Therapists. You can find referrals for family mediators, parenting coordinators, special masters, and coparenting specialists by asking your counselor or family law attorney for the names of professionals they have worked with themselves. Often your local Family Service Agency and Legal Aid organizations are able to be of service.

Appendix 3

Safety Rules

• • • • • • • • • • • • • • • • • •

IDEAS TO CONSIDER WHEN YOU
MAKE UP YOUR OWN LIST

Safety At Home And Away

- Always get permission from parents to leave the house. Tell them where you are going and who you will be with, how the parent can reach you, and when you will return.

- Always use the safety belt when riding in a car.

- Always wear a helmet when riding bicycles, skateboards, and

  _____

- (Names)_____ must always be in the company of an adult or _____(older child).

- (Names)_____ may not use the stove, toaster, knives, or _____ without an adult present.

- You are not allowed to play with guns, knives, or sticks—real or fake.

- You must always get permission to ride in someone else's car.

  * Do not open the door to anyone we do not know well. Always find a parent who will decide whether to open the door or not.

  * Electronics must be turned off before you leave the house or when you go to bed.

  * All equipment must be turned off and toys put away at bedtime.

House Security

All doors and windows are to be kept locked during _____AM _____PM.

EMERGENCIES

See *Appendix 8: Important Phone Numbers, Safety and Emergency Hotlines*

Combinations to locks and codes are secret and are never shared with others outside of the family. This includes computer and Internet passwords.

INTERNET AND ELECTRONIC SAFETY RULES

Today a parent's job is much more than just blocking certain sites or limiting phone usage. They have to help their child get smart about the Internet, their cell phones, and e-tablets. We can't be with our children every second monitoring what they do, read, or see, but we can teach them how to develop good judgment and when to tell us about something they see or hear. As important as social networking can be, the downside is that anyone can write things that are not true and post and view any video or photo. This is lawless territory where anything goes and everything remains on your internet "record." It can be devastating to a child if he or she either becomes part of a risky cyber-crowd or becomes a target of humiliation, bullying, or is solicited by a clever predator. The bottom line. Make some internet and electronic safety rules and follow through with them.

Internet Safety Guide: Here is a resource where parents can pick up easy-to-use internet safety rules for their children: *www.commonsense. com/internet-safety-guide*.

Electronics and Driving: Have a rule that there should be no texting, tweeting, or talking on the phone when driving. Research shows how dangerous it is, especially for teens. Although it is hard to enforce such a rule when you are not with your teenage driver, you can still make the rule, enforce it when you see it, and practice the rule yourself. Here is a resource where parents can pick up easy-to-use safety rules for their children: *www.commonsense.com/internet-safety-guide*.

Appendix 4

House Rules

• • • • • • • • • • • • • • • • • •

Reminder: When parents have a good routine and clear expectations, these can go a long way to help the kids feel safer and more secure—especially during transitions. Even though kids will be kids and there will be arguments and upsets, everyone is better off knowing the way they should treat one another and themselves.

HOUSE RULES EXAMPLE

Have your rules describe who you are as a family and what you stand for. The rules here are just an example. You should write your own version.

OUR FAMILY

We are a team. We take care of one another.

We will treat each other with respect and support one another. We do not allow behaviors such as rudeness, lying, hurtful teasing, bad language, kicking, punching, throwing things, hitting, scratching, screaming, calling names, scaring pets or people, threatening to hurt someone or something, stealing, not following our family rules, or _____). (Parents, change this list to suit you and your family.)

OUR HOME

We will all treat our home—inside and out—with care and respect. This includes everyone's own private property. We will respect each other's privacy and not go into each other's rooms or things without permission. When leaving your room, turn off the lights.

OUR PETS

We will treat our pets kindly and keep them healthy.

BEDTIME

- (Name) _____ School nights: ___ PM   Weekends ___ PM
- (Name) _____ School nights: ___ PM   Weekends ___ PM
- (Name) _____ School nights: ___ PM   Weekends ___ PM

MEALS

- Breakfast (time)_____
- Dinner time (time)_____

BEFORE SCHOOL

_____ AM   Ready for school
_____ AM   Out the door

AFTER SCHOOL

Getting home (pickups, carpools, buses) _____
Homework (times) _____
Family work (such as laundry, trash, walk dog, feed birds/cats/fish/
    dog) _____.

YOUR THINGS AND FAMLY AREAS

Return items to their place or to their owner when you are through using
them.

YOUR CLOTHES AND YOUR GROOMING

Dress neatly every day with clean clothes. Put dirty clothes in the hamper.
Take a bath or a shower every day.

COMPUTER AND INTERNET

Parents, you may want to write out when the child can use the computer,
phones, iPads, eTablets, for homework or surfing and when for socializing
with games, social networking sites, YouTube, music, and so forth. You
might also repeat that when they are on the Internet, they have to follow

all the parents' rules. In *Appendix 3: Safety Rules*, you could list your Internet rules in detail and even name the sites that are off-limits. Given the way things change, you would probably have to update this list frequently.

ELECTRONIC GAMES

As parents you can set limits on how your child uses these electronics. List number of hours, specific games, etc.

FAMILY WORK

Everyone is expected to do their share of the family's work. The chore schedules are posted.

PHONES

Ask for parents' permission before using the home office phone.
Cell Phones: _____
Overcharges: _____
When cell phones should be turned off: _____

FAMILY MEETINGS

Family meetings (one parent and the children <u>or</u> both parents and children) are held (once a week/2 weeks/monthly, when needed) _____
_____

Topic ideas: coordinate schedules, discuss vacation and activity plans, meal plans, vacation plans, household chore schedules, supporting a family member with a goal or a personal issue, family time, allowances/ finance review, problems to solve, make a list of our family values (see Appendix 5 for sample family values), etc.

ADDITIONS, WRITE IN _____
_____
_____
_____
_____

Things to Consider When Making Rules for Teens

Tip: If you have younger children, do you want these rules for your teen to be private or shared with the entire family?

What do you want to say to your teen about driving? Will an officer's warning about speeding be enough to take away the keys? Should kids ride in cars with classmates or older teens? What about riding motorcycles, off-road vehicles, conditions for attending parties, your expectations regarding alcohol, marijuana, other drugs, sex? If you haven't already done so, it probably wouldn't hurt to add these along with how to share costs for gas, managing allowances, checking accounts, saving accounts, budgets, part-time jobs, credit cards, bus passes, cars, cell phones, extra charges, sports equipment, musical instruments, concert and activity tickets, bikes, downloads (especially games), software, and apps.

Appendix 5
Example List of Family Values

• • • • • • • • • • • • • • • • • •

Here's a simple list to get you thinking what values you want to put in writing for you and your children.

IN OUR FAMILY,

We are a family team.
We care deeply about each other.
We protect one another.
We respect and trust each other.
We are honest with each other.
We help one another solve problems.
We do not hurt each other with words or violence.
We consider the other person's feelings.
We are courteous and kind with each other.
We work together and support each other.
Everyone does their part for the family and keeping up our home.

Appendix 6

Holiday Tips for Separated or Divorced Parents and Blended Families

● ● ● ● ● ● ● ● ● ● ● ● ● ● ● ● ● ●

1. **What's really important?** Ask your children, "What are your favorite things about the holidays?" Children need to feel they have a voice and can talk about what's really important to them. Asking this question can bring you closer together and provide you with the opportunity to let them express their feelings. Even if you no longer can afford that holiday or vacation ski trip or a big shopping spree, you can still do lower-budget fun things.

2. **Remember, your children take their cues from you.** Kids interpret events based on their parents' attitudes and actions. When the children are with you, try not to feel guilty or angry about the divorce or the way the children's time is arranged. Instead, try your best to appreciate what you do have that's precious. Health? Togetherness? Slowing down during the holiday break? A family team? Friends and family?

3. **Work together to plan and produce holiday traditions.** After separation, the "old family feeling" needs to be reshaped into your "new family feeling." Working together as a team for a party or to prepare for a religious service can be a powerful healer. Mom or Dad can be the family team leader in their home, but the kids should also feel ownership of the way they do their part. Everyone can enjoy!

4. **Concentrate on things that are not high-budget.** Separation or divorce rarely leaves enough money for everyone to do everything they desire. But the ads and hype around the holidays can feel like everyone can afford new electronics, clothes, trips, and parties. When these are out of reach, it can leave you feeling deprived, even depressed. Take a reality check. Is acquiring material things the only key to happy holidays? Help your children appreciate the lasting pleasures of friendship, giving to others less fortunate, homemade gifts, and giving the gift of oneself.

THE COPARENTING **TOOLKIT** BY ISOLINA RICCI

5. **Plan now and doublecheck your plans with others.** Contact the other parent and doublecheck the time, place, and details of how this holiday season will work for the kids. Don't put this off. A parent might assume that the transition takes place after Thanksgiving dinner at 3 p.m., but the other parent assumes that the children will eat dinner with them later. Even if you already have a Parenting Plan with holiday dates and times, reconfirm the transition times, where and when and which one of you picks up or drops off. Holidays are notorious for confused signals.

6. **Set some limits and take care of yourself.** Think back to last year. Did you or one of the kids get sick because you overdid it and there was not enough sleep or down-time? The holidays can be too much and our bodies don't like it. Children especially are creatures of routine. All the holiday "exceptions" like late bedtimes, extra sweets, travel, or outings, can eventually backfire and lead to irritability, illness, or exhaustion.

Finally, if you feel that deep ache in the pit of your stomach because of all that's happened with the divorce and your children, try to take some deep breaths and reach out to others for understanding. Take heart, things do get better over time. There is a way through this to a better day.

Appendix 7

When and When Not to Use the Traditional "I" Message

• • • • • • • • • • • • • • • • • •

Pick and Choose When to Use It!*

This is a formula for close friends and intimates—people who should or could care about how you feel. It is a way of using words to help defuse conflict and misunderstandings by revealing how you feel about something another person has said or done. It is designed to help both people appreciate how their actions affect others. The hope is that the person learning about your reactions will act better toward you and take responsibility for the impact of their behavior on you.

Traditional Formula
Express your Emotions

When you _____ (describe the other person's tone, words, or action),
I feel _____ (identify your feeling),
because _____ (explain in a few words).

Example: boyfriend to girlfriend: "When you use that tone of voice with me, I feel put down because it sounds like you think I'm stupid."

When "I" Messages Are Useful, Helpful:

- Adult to adult in relationships where they want to become emotionally closer.

- Child to child in attempts to defuse smaller misunderstandings.

- Child to parent (not parent to child) in trying to explain how a parent's behavior makes him or her feel and why.

When "I" Messages Are
Not Useful and Can Backfire:

- With coparents or former partners
- Bullies
- Parent to child
- Business associates
- Acquaintances
- People who don't care how you feel

IMPORTANT NOTE: I do not recommend that a parent use the emotional type of "I" messages with their child. You are the adult. Your child is not responsible for how you feel. Be direct. Don't say, "When you talk back to me that way, I feel hurt and discouraged." This gives the child the impression that they are responsible for your feelings, that you want them to change out of pity or respect for you. This blurs the boundaries between parent and child. You alone are responsible for how you feel and how you react.

Instead, be the parent, the family leader, and mentor. Example: "I do not want you to speak to me with that tone of voice. It is not good for you to talk like that to me or anyone. It is disrespectful and rude."

*A special thanks to Jane Bluestein, Ph.D., for her work with "I" messages. See "What's Wrong with I-Messages," and "Magic Sentences," available online at www.JaneBluestein.com.

Appendix 8

Important Phone Numbers, Safety and Emergency Hotlines

• • • • • • • • • • • • • • • • • •

Call 911 for Dangerous or Disturbing Situations
Give them your name, our address, phone number

Call parents:

Mom's cell _____ work number _____ other _____

Dad's cell _____ work number _____ other _____

Other _____

Neighbors, friends, family:

(name and number) _____

(name and number) _____

(name and number) _____

(name and number) _____

(name and number) _____

Sheriff _____

Local Police Station _____

Doctors _____

_____

_____

_____

_____

Pediatrician _____

Veterinarian _____

Closest Emergency Room _____

_____

National Sexual Assault Hotline: 1-800-656-HOPE

Poison Control Hotline: 1-800-222-1222

National Suicide Prevention Hotline: 1-800-273-TALK

National Child Abuse Hotline: 1-800-4-A-CHILD

Appendix 9

When You Have Done All You Can Do

• • • • • • • • • • • • • • • • • •

Coparenting is supposed to develop into a healthy situation for everyone. But sometimes, despite your efforts, coparenting is not healthy and people suffer—especially the children. This may be because of conflict between the parents, because of the actions of one parent, or poor parenting. Perhaps one parent doesn't follow the Agreement or loses interest in being an active parent. Maybe someone is addicted to negative intimacy and the kids are still caught in the middle. Perhaps there are financial, emotional, or physical health problems, or someone has been dishonest or has attempted to alienate the children.

There can be many reasons why things don't work out, but the bottom line is that when coparenting becomes a liability to the kids, to you, or to the family, things have to change for the better. But how?

What are your options? Throughout this book, there have been suggestions to seek expert help when limited coparenting has gone on too long or there are other roadblocks or big problems. Before you decide whether or not to go to court, get some expert support. First consider family mediation and coparent counseling. When mediation and coparent counseling are successful, people learn to hear each other again and are more open to rebuilding mutual respect. A mediator guides them to making decisions about their parenting plan and parenting time. But when conflict is especially high, mediation may not work. To be effective it needs parents to have a level of mutual trust and an openness to compromise.

If you work with a coparent counselor, you may find a way to negotiate a cease-fire or a time-out for a few weeks so you can focus on the needs of the children and those of the entire family. Ordinarily, a counselor will not make any decisions for you, but he or she may make recommendations about the children that you may choose to follow or not.

Ask your attorney or counselor about how child custody evaluators, parenting coordinators, and special masters work with families in your local area. Engaging one of these professionals is a very serious commitment of time and expense and may require filing some court documents.

However, these professionals can do things mediators and counselors cannot do. If asked, a child custody evaluator can address the question, "What parenting arrangement for this family is healthy for these children?" However, once the evaluation is complete, the evaluator no longer works with the family. However, the parenting coordinator or a special master works with the family on an ongoing basis. They may make decisions for you when you can't agree.

Be advised: Not everyone believes that a child custody evaluation, a parenting coordinator, or a special master is ultimately the best solution. Learn as much as you can about these options before you go ahead.

A final step is to work with an attorney to address the major issues between you and the other parent in a formal, legal way. Your efforts, even if they are successful, don't guarantee that the fighting will stop or that it will be healthier for everyone. For some people, going to court does settle an issue and it seems to be a relief; for others, however, it only complicates things further.

Whatever you decide to do, you must keep your children away from the conflict, and continue to be the very best parent you can be. If doing this is too difficult, then please consider individual therapy or counseling for you and the children. As has been said many times before in this book, open conflict and underlying hostility between parents is deeply destructive. A personal counselor may help you find ways to shield yourself and the children from its worst effects.

Finally, even if a standard coparenting arrangement is not right for you now, life has a way of bringing along even more changes and challenges after divorce, especially when we least expect them. Perhaps something will happen that will enable you to work together again. Then you can give your children the best of both of your worlds.

Take care.

Appendix 10

The Bookshelf

• • • • • • • • • • • • • • • • • •

A Sample of Available Children's Books

A Smart Girl's Guide to Her Parents' Divorce: How to Land on Your Feet When Your World Turns Upside Down by Nancy Holyoke and Scott Nash, American Girl Library, 2009

Dinosaurs Divorce by Marc Brown and Laurie Krasny, Little, Brown Books for Young Readers, 1988

Mom's House, Dad's House for Kids: Feeling at Home in One Home or Two by Isolina Ricci, Fireside Books, 2006

Standing on My Own Two Feet: A Child's Affirmation of Love in the Midst of Divorce by Tamara Schmitz, Price Stern Sloan, 2008

Two Homes by Claire Masurel (author) and Kady MacDonald Denton (illustrator), Candlewick, 2003

What in the World Do You Do When Your Parents Divorce? A Survival Guide for Kids by Kent Winchester, J.D., and Roberta Beyer, J.D., Free Spirit Publishing, 2001

A Sample of Books for Parents

I strongly encourage readers to make use of various self-help books and seminars on parenting and coparenting. Although books, podcasts, videos, and audios are not substitutes for therapy or classes for parent education, they can still be very helpful.

Difficult Questions Kids Ask and Are Afraid to Ask about Divorce by Meg F. Schneider and Joan Zuckerberg, Fireside Books, 1996

Helping Your Kids Cope with Divorce the Sandcastles Way by M. Gary Neuman and Patricia Romanowski, Random House, 1999

Mom's House, Dad's House: Making Two Homes for Your Child by Isolina Ricci, Ph.D., Fireside Books, 2nd edition, 1997

Mom's House, Dad's House for Kids: Feeling at Home in One Home or Two by Isolina Ricci, Fireside Books, 2006

Positive Discipline from A to Z by Jane Nelson, Three Rivers Press, 2007

Positive Discipline for Single Parents by Jane Nelson, Three Rivers Press, 2nd edition, 1999

Splitting: Protecting Yourself While Divorcing Someone with Borderline or Narcissistic Personality Disorder by Bill Eddy, New Harbinger Publications, 2011

The Good Divorce by Constance Ahrons, Ph.D., Harper Paperbacks, 1995

The Heart of Parenting: Raising an Emotionally Intelligent Child by John Gottman, Ph.D., with Joan DeClaire, Simon & Schuster, 1997

The Optimistic Child: A Proven Program to Safeguard Children against Depression and Build Lifelong Resilience by Martin E. P. Seligman, Ph.D., with Karen Reivich, Ph.D., Lisa Jaycox, Ph.D., and Jane Gillham, Ph.D., Houghton Mifflin, 1995, 2007

The Special Needs Child and Divorce by Margaret "Pegi" S. Price, American Bar Association, 2009

The Truth about Children and Divorce: Dealing with the Emotions So You and Your Children Can Thrive by Robert E. Emery, Ph.D., Plume Books, 2006

The Whole-Brain Child, by Daniel J. Siegel, M.D. and Tina P Bryson, Ph.D., Delacorte Press, 2011.

We're Still Family by Constance Ahrons, Ph.D., Harper Paperbacks, 2005

Thank You

• • • • • • • • • • • • • • • • • •

Many wise professionals and parents have contributed to this book. I can name only a few here. I am deeply grateful for their willingness to share their wisdom, insights, and experience. A special thank-you to the mental health professionals, mediators, and attorneys who generously gave of their time to review and comment on various stages of this book, especially to Cathy Lyman, Liz Salin, Louise Lee, Debra Pontisso, Phil Reedy, Lorraine Sanchez, Linda Delbar, and Andrew and Michelle Firstman. I also want to thank all the other professionals who offered their insights and suggestions during my workshops and trainings.

A heartfelt thanks to those who helped bring all the pieces together for the production of this book: my editor, Kathleen Erickson, for her saintly patience, wisdom, expertise, and treasured friendship; Eric Elfman for his eagle eye and excellent suggestions; Michael Rohani of Design for Books for making this book easy to read and great to look at, and to Amy Garrett for her creative suggestions and concepts.

I save my deepest gratitude and appreciation for all the parents and children it has been my privilege to know and work with over more than 30 years. They brought their courage, commitment, ingenuity, and love for their children to the task of reorganizing their lives. Thank you all for sharing your experiences with me.

About the Author

Isolina Ricci, Ph.D., author of the enduring classic for parents *Mom's House, Dad's House*, and *Mom's House, Dad's House for KIDS*, is an internationally renowned licensed family therapist, educator, and mediator whose work has inspired and supported two generations of separated, divorced, and remarried parents and their children.

Many of her pioneering concepts such as "Parenting Plans," the "business-like" approach, and better words to replace legal terms like "custody" and "visitation," have become accepted standards. Her work has been cited in courtrooms, classrooms, and legal publications. In addition to her work with families, she headed the Statewide Office of Family Court Services for the California courts for 15 years and conducted research on divorce and child adjustment at Stanford University. She is the recipient of the Distinguished Mediator Award from the Academy of Family Mediators, and Distinguished Service Awards from both the International and California Association of Family and Conciliation Courts for her outstanding contributions and achievements.

Dr. Ricci is the founder and director of Custody & CoParenting Solutions and CoParentingToday.com (formerly known as The New Family Center). She divides her time between school visits, and conducting seminars and trainings for professionals.

Visit her at
www.coparentingtoday.com and
www.thecoparentingtoolkit.com.

30995115R00110

Made in the USA
Middletown, DE
14 April 2016